SCHOLASTIC

The BIG Book of
Pocket Chart Poems
ABCs & 123s

by Linda B. Ross

New York • Toronto • London • Auckland • Sydney
Mexico City • New Delhi • Hong Kong • Buenos Aires

Teaching
Resources

Edited by Joan Novelli.
Cover design by Brian LaRossa.
Interior design by Holly Grundon.
Interior art by Maxie Chambliss.

ISBN-13: 978-0-439-51385-2
ISBN-10: 0-439-51385-5

1 2 3 4 5 6 7 8 9 10   40   15 14 13 12 11 10 09 08 07

Contents

Alphabet Lessons

Number Lessons

Welcome to *The Big Book of Pocket Chart Poems: ABCs & 123s*! This book contains everything you need to teach the alphabet and the numbers 1–30, including 48 engaging and easy-to-follow lesson plans that use poems and pictures as a springboard for teaching each letter and number. Lessons for each letter of the alphabet include letter identification, letter-sound relationships, and letter formation. Lessons for numbers 1–30 feature number identification and matching activities, counting practice, and number formation. Both sets of lessons feature a mini-book children can complete to practice essential skills introduced in the lessons.

Pocket charts provide an interactive format for teaching the alphabet and number concepts. Your students become active participants as they identify and use the letters, words, and pictures for each alphabet poem, and the numbers, pictures, and counters for each number poem. After you complete a lesson, display the pocket chart with the day's poem and manipulatives (letter and picture cards for ABC lessons; number and picture cards and counters for number lessons) in your reading and math learning centers to provide ongoing practice.

A Look at the Alphabet Lessons

Each alphabet lesson features a playful pocket chart poem that teaches essential letter-sound relationships through rhyme and repetition. Pages 12–78 feature lesson plans for each letter of the alphabet (including separate lessons for short- and long-vowel sounds), and additional activities and games for use with any letter. Each of these lesson plans includes complete instructions for setting up and teaching with the pocket chart rhyme, and the following reproducible materials:

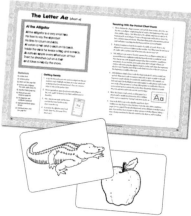

- alphabet frame (for isolating target letters in the pocket chart poems; page 83)

- letter and picture cards (pages 79–109)

- interactive alphabet mini-book (pages 110–111)

- letter strips for customizing the mini-book (pages 112–117)

Tip

When preparing picture cards and counters for use with letter and number pocket chart lessons, consider coloring them for added visual appeal, and laminating them for durability.

Making and Using the Alphabet Mini-Books

Customize the mini-book for each lesson as follows:

Step 1 (cover): Glue the "letter formation" strip (page 112) for the target letter in the space provided. Or, write the target letter (uppercase and lowercase), using arrows to show formation.

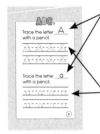

Step 2 (page 2): Write the target letter (uppercase and lowercase) in the spaces provided.

Step 3 (page 2): Glue the uppercase and lowercase "tracing" strips (pages 113–117) in the spaces provided. Or, write the letters (with a light or dashed line) for children to trace.

Step 4 (page 3): Write the target letter (uppercase and lowercase) for children to use as a model for practicing the letter on their own.

Step 5 (page 4): Write the target letter. If desired write a word on the line from the corresponding rhyme that features the target letter, and have children practice writing it. Or, have them copy words directly from the pocket chart poem.

To complete the mini-books, guide children in following these directions:

Page 1: Trace the letter with your finger.

Page 2: Trace the letter with a pencil.

Page 3: Write the letter.

Page 4: Write words with the letter. (Children can copy words from the pocket chart poem.) On the back of page 4 (or on a separate sheet of paper), draw a picture about the letter.

About Consonant and Vowel Sounds

This book is designed to provide instruction for the letters of the alphabet and the sounds most commonly associated with those letters, including the sounds represented by individual consonants and the long and short sounds represented by vowels. However, there are many other sounds that letters can represent.

❖ The letter *c*, for example, generally stands for the /k/ sound when it comes before the letter *a*, *o*, or *u* in a word (*cat, cook, cup*). It generally stands for the /s/ sound when it comes before the letter *e*, *i*, or *y* in a word (*cent, cider, cycle*). The letter *g* can also have more than one sound, but most often it represents the "hard g" sound in *goose* or *goat*. In this book, the poems for the letters *c* and *g* focus on the *c* as in *cat* and the *g* as in *goose*.

continued

Tip

To distinguish between a letter (such as *a*) and a sound (such as the short-*a* sound in *hat*), please note the following: References to letters in this book are made in italicized print (*Aa*); sounds are represented by letters placed within slashes (/a/). A short-vowel sound is represented by the corresponding letter within slashes and no diacritical mark (for example, the /a/ sound in *hat*). The macron (¯) is used to represent long-vowel sounds (for example, the /ā/ sound in *plane*). For a special note about the long-*u* sound, please see page 63.

✿ Two consonants together can represent a single sound, known as a digraph. For example, together the letters *sh* make the /sh/ sound as in *shop*. Though some rhymes in this book include digraphs (such as *that*, *whales*, and *cherry*), the focus for consonants is on individual letters and the sounds they commonly represent.

✿ Vowels can also have a variety of sounds. For example, in addition to its short and long sound, the letter *a* can have the /ô/ sound as in *ball* or the schwa sound (ə) as in *again*, *above*, and *along*. These are known as variant vowel sounds. The letter *a* can also have an *r*-controlled sound (/är/) at the beginning of a word, as in *arm* and *art*, in the medial position, as in *harm* and *yard*, and in the final position, as in *car* and *hare*.

For ideas on extending the rhymes to teach additional sounds that letters make, please see page 10.

A Look at the Number Lessons

Each number lesson features a playful pocket chart poem for teaching essential understanding of whole numbers, including number recognition, concepts of correspondence, and counting. Pages 118–154 feature lesson plans for the numbers 1–30, and additional activities and games for use with any number. Each of these lesson plans includes complete instructions for setting up and teaching with the pocket chart rhyme, and the following reproducible materials:

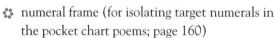

✿ numeral frame (for isolating target numerals in the pocket chart poems; page 160)

✿ numeral and picture cards (pages 155–170)

✿ counters (page 176)

✿ interactive mini-book for reinforcing number skills and concepts (pages 171–172)

✿ numeral strips for customizing the mini-book for each number (pages 173–175)

Making and Using the Number Mini-Books

Customize the mini-book for each lesson as follows:

Step 1 (cover): Glue the "numeral formation" strip (page 173) for the target numeral in the space provided on the cover. Or, write the target numeral, using arrows to show formation.

Step 2 (page 2): Write the target numeral in the spaces provided.

Step 3 (page 2): Glue the numeral "tracing" strip (pages 173–175) in the space provided. Or, write the numeral (with a light or dashed line) for children to trace.

Step 4 (page 3): Write the target numeral.

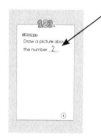

Step 5 (page 4): Write the target numeral.

To complete the mini-books, guide children in following these directions:

Page 1: Trace the numeral with your finger.

Page 2: Trace and write the numeral.

Page 3: Paste the corresponding number of counters in the mini-book.

Page 4 (or a separate sheet of paper): Draw a picture about the number.

Practicing Letter and Numeral Formation

Each lesson includes instruction in letter and numeral formation. As you write the target letter or numeral on chart paper (or a whiteboard), invite children to follow your movements to practice the formation themselves. As suggested in the lessons, children can do this by using their finger to "write" the letter or numeral in the air, on a partner's back, or on the palm of their hand. Following are other suggestions to add variety to this portion of the lessons:

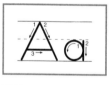

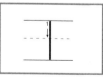

❖ Children can use their finger to write the letter or numeral on their table area.

❖ Invite children to dip a finger in water, then write the letter or numeral on a chalkboard.

❖ Let children practice writing the letter or numeral in a little shaving cream that you have squirted on their desk or table area. (Soapsuds work well, too.)

Research Connections

Alphabet Lessons

Rhyme is an effective way to introduce children to the sounds of words. "Sensitivity to rhyme comes quite easily to most children. For that reason, rhyme play is an excellent entry to phonological awareness. Because rhyme play directs children's attention to similarities and differences in the sounds of words, it is a useful means of alerting them to the insight that language has not only meaning and message but also physical form." (Adams, et al.; 1998)

Al the Alligator · Aa

Al the alligator is a very smart lad.

He likes to say the alphabet.

He likes to count and add.

Al wears a hat and a pack on his back.

Inside the pack, he keeps a flag and a snack.

Al eats an apple every afternoon at four.

Then he stretches out on a mat

and takes a nap by the shore.

According to the report of the National Reading Panel, children who have phonemic awareness skills are likely to have an easier time learning to read and spell than children who have few or none of these skills. "Phonemic awareness is the understanding that there is a predictable relationship between phonemes and graphemes, the letters that represent those sounds in written language. Effective phonemic awareness instruction teaches children to notice, think about, and work with (manipulate) sounds in spoken language." (National Reading Panel, 2000)

Phonics instruction teaches the relationships between letters and sounds. It teaches children to utilize these relationships to read and write words. "The goal of phonics instruction is to help children learn and use the alphabetic principle—the understanding that there are systematic and predictable relationships between written letters and spoken sounds. In short, knowledge of the alphabetic principle contributes greatly to children's ability to read words both in isolation and in connected text." (National Reading Panel, 2000)

Number Lessons

Experts agree that preschool students have significant mathematical strengths. "In particular, it appears that young children—despite important limitations—are capable of understanding much more about number and arithmetic than previously or commonly thought possible." (Baroody, 2003)

Using manipulatives helps children to explore number composition and develop number sense. According to Clements and McMillen (1996), "Most students do not use manipulatives as often as needed. Thoughtful use can enhance almost every topic. Students must learn to use manipulatives as tools for thinking about mathematics."

Connections to the Standards

Language Arts

The lesson plans in this book support the following language arts standards outlined by Mid-continent Research for Education and Learning (McREL):

- Discriminates among the sounds of spoken language.

- Knows rhyming sounds and simple rhymes.

- Knows that words are made up of sounds.

- Uses basic elements of phonetic analysis.

- Reads aloud familiar stories, poems, and passages with fluency and expression.

- Knows that print and written symbols convey meaning and represent spoken language.

- Understands that illustrations and pictures convey meaning.

- Knows that print is read from left to right, top to bottom.

- Listens for a variety of purposes.

- Gives and responds to oral directions.

- Knows that writing, including pictures, letters, and words, communicates meaning and information.

- Uses drawings to express thoughts, feelings, and ideas.

- Uses emergent writing skills to write for a variety of purposes and to write in a variety of forms.

- Uses knowledge of letters to write or copy familiar words.

- Uses phonic knowledge to spell simple words.

Math

The lesson plans in this book support the following math standards outlined by the National Council of Teachers of Mathematics (NCTM):

- Understands numbers, ways of representing numbers, relationships among numbers, and number systems.

- Understands meanings of operations and how they relate to one another.

- Computes fluently and makes reasonable estimates.

- Organizes and consolidates mathematical thinking through communication.

- Communicates mathematical thinking coherently and clearly to peers, teachers, and others.

- Uses the language of mathematics to express mathematical ideas precisely.

Extending the Lessons

As you use the pocket chart rhymes and lessons to teach letters and numbers, you'll find that opportunities naturally arise to teach other important and engaging lessons. For example, each poem's rhyming structure creates opportunities to teach phonograms. In addition to using "5 Little Chicks" (page 126) to teach the number five, use this rhyme to teach the short-*i* phonogram -*ick*, the short-*a* phonogram -*ack*, or the long-*a* phonogram -*ay*. Here's a sampling of similar opportunities you'll find throughout the letter and number lessons:

❧ "Under an Umbrella" (page 60): In this rhyme for the letter *Uu*, three animal friends huddle *under* an umbrella and jump *across* a puddle. After completing the lesson, revisit the rhyme to help children learn more about prepositions such as these. Use the picture cards to show, for example, Duck *in front of* the puddle, Cub *between* Duck and Pup, or three friends splashing *in* the puddle! (This rhyme is also fun for teaching "consonant + le" words, such as *huddle* and *puddle*.)

❧ "Six Little Inchworms" (page 32): After teaching the letter *Ii*, you might take a few minutes to investigate this caterpillar's name and explore the concept of an inch. Of course, this rhyme is also perfect for teaching about the number 6!

❧ "2 of a Kind" (page 120): After using the rhyme to explore things that come in twos, use the words *run*, *hop*, *skip*, and *jump* to introduce action verbs, and the idea that these words help readers create specific pictures in their minds. Invite children to act out the action words in the last two lines of the rhyme, then brainstorm other words that tell how they can move.

❧ "10 Turtles Racing" (page 136): After using the rhyme to teach the number 10, use it to explore adjectives that compare, such as *fastest* (from the rhyme) and *slowest*. What other words can compare people, places, things, or ideas? Make a math connection at the same time with size-order words. Children can arrange the animals from the rhyme in order by size and use words to compare them: turtle (*big*), rabbit (*bigger*), and bear (*biggest*).

❧ "Can a Cat Do That?" (page 18): This poem for the letter *Cc* asks questions about what a cat can do. After completing the lesson, you can use the poem as a springboard for teaching or reinforcing the concepts of real and make-believe. Discuss with children the nonfiction books they have read about cats and other animals and the fantasy books they have read that feature animal characters. Draw a T-chart on chart paper, and list titles for the two categories of books.

❖ "Eddie Elephant" (page 22): After teaching the letter *Ee* and the short *e* sound, use the poem to teach the /ch/ sound of the digraph *ch*, which appears at the beginning of the word *cherry* and at the end of the word *French*. Invite children to think of other words that begin or end with *ch*, such as *chick, chair, chart*, and *chop* or *lunch, bench, branch*, and *much*.

❖ "1 Cat Named Nat" (page 118): In addition to using this rhyme to teach the number 1, you can use it to introduce contractions. Point out the contractions *He's* (line 3) and *It's* (line 10). Explain that *He's* and *It's* are short forms for *He is* and *It is*. Point out that the apostrophe replaces the letter *i*. Then list other contractions on chart paper, such as *I'm, she's, we're, can't*, and *don't*. Have children identify the two words that form each contraction and the letter that was replaced by an apostrophe.

❖ "4 Funny Monkeys" (page 124): After using the poem to teach the number 4, you might take a few minutes to teach the sounds of the digraphs *th* and *wh* in the words *they* and *what*. Point out that the /th/ sound can be heard at the beginning of words such as *they, the, them, this*, and *that*. Point out also that the digraph *th* can stand for the /th/ sound that is heard at the beginning of words such as *thank, thin, thirteen*, and *think*. Explain that the digraph *wh* stands for the /hw/ sound that is heard at the beginning of words such as *what, whale, when*, and *why*.

Bibliography

Adams, M. J., Foorman, B. R., Lundberg, I. & Beeler, T. (1998). *Phonemic awareness in young children*. Baltimore, MD: Paul H. Brookes Publishing Co.

Baroody, A. (2004). The role of psychological research in the development of early childhood mathematics standards. In D. H. Clements, J. Sarama & A. DiBiase (Eds.), *Engaging young children in mathematics: Standards for early childhood mathematics education*. (pp. 149-172). Mahwah, N.J.: Lawrence Erlbaum Associates.

Clements, D. H. & McMillen, S. (1996). Rethinking concrete manipulatives. In *Teaching children mathematics, 2 (5), 270-279*. Reston, VA: National Council of Teachers of Mathematics.

Kendall, J. S. & Marzano, R. J. (2004). *Content knowledge: A compendium of standards and benchmarks for K-12 education*. Aurora, CO: Mid-continent Research for Education and Learning. Online database: http://www.mcrel.org/standards-benchmarks/.

National Council of Teachers of Mathematics (2006). *Curriculum focal points for prekindergarten through grade 8 mathematics*. Reston, VA: National Council of Teachers of Mathematics.

National Council of Teachers of Mathematics (2000). *Principles and standards for school mathematics*. Reston, VA: National Council of Teachers of Mathematics.

National Institute of Child Health and Human Development (2000). *Report of the National Reading Panel. Teaching children to read: An evidence-based assessment of the scientific research literature on reading and its implications for reading instruction: Reports of the subgroups* (NIH Publication No. 00-4754). Washington, D.C.: U.S. Government Printing Office.

The Letter Aa (short a)

Al the Alligator

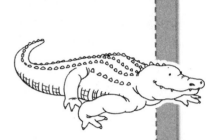

Al the **a**lligator is a very smart l**a**d.

He likes to say the **a**lphabet.

He likes to count **a**nd **a**dd.

Al wears a h**a**t **a**nd a s**a**ck on his b**a**ck.

Inside the s**a**ck he keeps a fl**a**g **a**nd a sn**a**ck.

Al eats **a**n **a**pple every **a**fternoon **a**t four.

Then he stretches out on a m**a**t

And takes a n**a**p by the shore.

Materials

❀ pocket chart

❀ sentence strips

❀ letter card (*Aa*; page 79)

❀ picture cards (alligator, hat, sack, apple; page 84)

❀ alphabet frame (page 83)

❀ blank picture card template (page 83)

❀ old magazines and workbooks (optional)

❀ alphabet mini-book (pages 110–111)

❀ mini-book letter strips (*Aa*; pages 112–113)

Getting Ready

1. Copy the title and poem onto sentence strips (one line per sentence strip). Highlight the letter *Aa* in the initial and medial position (as indicated above). Place the sentence strips in order in the pocket chart.

2. Photocopy and cut apart the picture cards (alligator, hat, sack, apple). If desired, color them and laminate for durability.

3. Place the picture cards and the letter card (in that order) in the pocket chart across the top.

4. Customize the alphabet mini-book for the letter *Aa*. (See page 5 for directions.)

Teaching With the Pocket Chart Poem

1. Point to the picture card for *alligator*, and ask children to name what they see. Say the word *alligator*, emphasizing the /a/ sound at the beginning of the word. Have children repeat. Ask: *What letter of the alphabet makes the /a/ sound at the beginning of the word* alligator? Point to the uppercase and lowercase *Aa*; have children name each letter. Then have them look at the remaining picture cards and name something else that begins with the /a/ sound (apple).

2. Explain: *Sometimes we hear the /a/ sound in the middle of a word.* Point to the picture cards for *hat* and *sack* and have children say the words. Ask: *What sound do you hear in the middle of the words* hat *and* sack? (/a/) *What letter makes the /a/ sound?* (a)

3. Tell children to get ready to listen to a poem about an alligator named Al. As you read the poem, emphasize words that have the initial or medial /a/ sound. Place the picture cards alongside corresponding lines to reinforce sound-letter associations. As you read the poem again, pause after each pair of lines. Let children take turns using the alphabet frame to isolate each letter *a* that represents the /a/ sound. Together, read all the words aloud and notice if the /a/ sound is at the beginning or in the middle of the word.

4. Ask children to think of new words that begin with /a/ and the letter *a*, such as *animal, ant,* and *ask.* Write new words on sentence strips, and cut apart to make word cards. Repeat for words with the /a/ sound in the medial position—for example, *cat, land,* and *map.* Use the blank picture card template to make picture cards for the new words. (Draw pictures or cut from old magazines or workbooks.) Place the new word and picture cards in the pocket chart. Encourage children to revisit the poem, pictures, and words over the next few days.

5. Write the letters A and *a* slowly on chart paper (or a whiteboard) to model their formation. Have children follow your movements by writing each letter in the air.

6. Give each child a copy of the alphabet mini-book. Have children use their finger to trace the letter *Aa* in the title. After completing pages 2–4 (see page 5 for directions), invite children to use the back of page 4 (or another sheet of paper) to draw a picture of Al the alligator taking a nap or doing something else that reinforces the letter *a*, such as feeding a cat.

The Letter Aa (long a)

Painting Pictures

I have some **pai**nt and a **pai**ntbrush too,

So I'll **pai**nt some pictures just for you!

I'll **pai**nt a pl**ane** in a big blue sky.

I'll **pai**nt a tr**ai**n as it r**a**c**e**s by.

I'll **pai**nt two wh**ale**s that pl**ay** in the sea.

Then I'll **pai**nt a picture of you and me!

Materials

❁ pocket chart

❁ sentence strips

❁ letter card (*Aa*; page 79)

❁ picture cards (paint, paintbrush, plane, train, whales; pages 85–86)

❁ blank picture card template (page 83)

❁ old magazines and workbooks (optional)

❁ alphabet mini-book (pages 110–111)

❁ mini-book letter strips (*Aa*; pages 112–113)

Getting Ready

1. Copy the title and poem onto sentence strips (one line per sentence strip). Highlight the letters that make the long-*a* sound (as indicated above). Place the sentence strips in order in the pocket chart.

2. Photocopy and cut apart the picture cards (paint, paintbrush, plane, train, whales). If desired, color them and laminate for durability.

3. Place the picture cards and the letter card (in that order) in the pocket chart across the top.

4. Customize the alphabet mini-book for the letter Aa. (See page 5 for directions.)

Teaching With the Pocket Chart Poem

1. Point to the picture card for *paint*, and ask children to say the name of the picture. Say the word *paint* again, emphasizing the /ā/ sound, and have children repeat it. Then write the word *paint* on chart paper (or a whiteboard), and point out that the letters *ai* make the /ā/ sound, which is the long-*a* sound. Continue in the same way with the picture cards for *plane*, *train*, *whales*, and *play*, pointing out that the letters *a_e* and *ay* can also make the /ā/ sound.

2. Invite children to get ready to listen to a poem about someone who wants to paint pictures. As you read aloud the poem, emphasize the words that have a long-*a* sound as you track the print. Place the picture cards alongside corresponding lines to reinforce sound-letter associations. When you read the poem a second time, pause after each line. Let children take turns coming to the chart to point to and say each word that has a long-*a* sound. Together, read all the words aloud.

3. Ask children to think of other words with the long-*a* sound—for example, *Kate*, *page*, *rain*, *name*, *cake*, and *hay*. Write their suggestions on sentence strips, trim to size, and place them in the pocket chart. Use the blank picture card template to make picture cards for the new words. (Draw pictures or cut from old magazines or workbooks.) Point out the letters in each word that form the long-*a* sound (*a_e*, *ai*, and *ay*). Keep the pocket chart on display so that children can revisit the poem, pictures, and words over the next few days.

4. Write the letters A and *a* slowly on chart paper (or a whiteboard) to model their formation. Have children follow your movements by writing each letter in the air.

5. Give each child a copy of the alphabet mini-book. Have children use their finger to trace the letter Aa in the title. After completing pages 2–4 (see page 5 for directions), invite children to use the back of page 4 (or another sheet of paper) to draw a picture about the letter Aa (and the /ā/ sound)—for example, a cake on a plate or a snake on a gate.

The Letter *Bb*

Bear and Butterfly

A **b**ear sat down **b**eneath a tree
To read his favorite **b**ook,
When a **b**utterfly came flying **b**y,
And asked to take a look.
Soon the **b**ear and **b**utterfly
Became the **b**est of friends.
Each **b**eautiful day they read and play,
And that's how this poem ends!

Materials

- pocket chart
- sentence strips
- letter card (*Bb*; page 79)
- picture cards (bear, book, butterfly; page 86)
- alphabet frame (page 83)
- blank picture card template (page 83)
- old magazines and workbooks (optional)
- alphabet mini-book (pages 110–111)
- mini-book letter strips (*Bb*; pages 112–113)

Getting Ready

1. Copy the title and poem onto sentence strips (one line per sentence strip). Highlight the letter *Bb* in the initial position (as indicated above). Place the sentence strips in order in the pocket chart.

2. Photocopy and cut apart the picture cards (bear, book, butterfly). If desired, color them and laminate for durability.

3. Place the picture cards and the letter card (in that order) in the pocket chart across the top.

4. Customize the alphabet mini-book for the letter *Bb*. (See page 5 for directions.)

Teaching With the Pocket Chart Poem

1. Begin by pointing to the picture card for *bear*. Invite children to tell what they see. Say the word *bear*, emphasizing the /b/ sound; have children repeat. Then ask what letter of the alphabet makes the /b/ sound. Point to the uppercase and lowercase *Bb* and have children name each letter. Ask them to identify the other pictures whose names begin with the /b/ sound and the letter *b* (book, butterfly).

2. Invite children to get ready to listen to a poem about a bear and a butterfly. As you read the poem, emphasize words that begin with the /b/ sound. Place the picture cards alongside corresponding lines to reinforce sound-letter associations. When you read the poem again, pause after each pair of lines. Have volunteers come to the chart and use the alphabet frame to isolate each letter *b* that begins a word and represents the /b/ sound. Read these words aloud with the group.

3. Ask children to think of other words that begin with the /b/ sound and the letter *b*—for example, *ball, balloon, banana, bicycle,* and *boat*. Write their suggestions on sentence strips, and trim to size. Make picture cards to match children's new words (using the blank picture card template and pictures you draw or cut from old magazines or workbooks). Place the new word and picture cards in the pocket chart. Keep the pocket chart on display so that children that can revisit the poem, pictures, and words over the next few days.

4. Write the letters *B* and *b* slowly on chart paper (or a whiteboard) to model their formation. Have children follow your movements by writing each letter in the air.

5. Give each child a copy of the alphabet mini-book. Have children use their finger to trace the letter *Bb* in the title. After completing pages 2–4 (see page 5 for directions), invite children to use the back of page 4 (or another sheet of paper) to draw a picture of the bear and the butterfly reading a book or trying something new together, such as riding a bike or playing ball.

The Letter Cc

Can a Cat Do That?

Can a **c**at tie a shoe?
That **c**an't be true!
Can a **c**at **c**ook a meal?
That **c**an't be real!
Can a **c**at learn to fly?
No, that's a big lie!
Can a **c**at love me?
Yes, that **c**an be!

Materials

- pocket chart
- sentence strips
- letter card (*Cc*; page 79)
- picture card (cat; page 87)
- alphabet frame (page 83)
- blank picture card template (page 83)
- old magazines and workbooks (optional)
- alphabet mini-book (pages 110–111)
- mini-book letter strips (*Cc*; pages 112–113)

Getting Ready

1. Copy the title and poem onto sentence strips (one line per sentence strip). Highlight the letter Cc in the initial position (as indicated above). Place the sentence strips in order in the pocket chart.

2. Photocopy and cut apart the picture card (cat). If desired, color it and laminate for durability.

3. Place the picture card and the letter card (in that order) in the pocket chart across the top.

4. Customize the alphabet mini-book for the letter Cc. (See page 5 for directions.)

Teaching With the Pocket Chart Poem

1. Begin by pointing to the picture card for *cat*, and ask children what they see. Say the word *cat*, emphasizing the /k/ sound; have children repeat it. Then ask what letter of the alphabet makes the /k/ sound. (If children know that the letter *k* also makes the /k/ sound, explain that both *c* and *k* make the /k/ sound.) Point to the uppercase and lowercase *Cc* and have children name each letter. Ask them to name something else in the picture that begins with the /k/ sound (collar).

2. Invite children to get ready to listen to a poem about the things a cat can and cannot do. As you read the poem, emphasize those words that begin with the /k/ sound. Place the picture card alongside one of the corresponding lines to reinforce sound-letter associations. When you read the poem again, pause after each pair of lines. Have volunteers use the alphabet frame to isolate each letter *c* that begins a word and represents the /k/ sound. Read the words aloud with the group.

3. Ask children to think of other words that begin with the /k/ sound, such as *corn*, *cow*, and *cookie*. List words on chart paper (or a whiteboard). Note that children might suggest words that begin with *k*; if so, make a second list of words that begin with *k*. Write words that begin with *c* on sentence strips, and trim to size. Make picture cards to match children's new words (using the blank picture card template and pictures you draw or cut from old magazines or workbooks). Place the new word and picture cards in the pocket chart. Keep the pocket chart on display so that children can revisit the poem, pictures, and words over the next few days.

4. Write the letters *C* and *c* slowly on chart paper (or a whiteboard) to model their formation. Have children follow your movements by using their finger to write each letter on their palm.

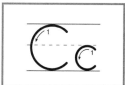

5. Give each child a copy of the alphabet mini-book. Have children use their finger to trace the letter *Cc* on the cover. After completing pages 2–4 (see page 5 for directions), invite children to use the back of page 4 (or another sheet of paper) to draw a picture of the cat with a collar drinking water from a cup. Children might also choose to draw the cat doing something else that represents the letter *Cc*, such as curling up on a coat or licking ice cream from a cone.

The Letter *Dd*

Dancing Deer

One **d**ay I saw a little **d**eer.
She had a **d**aisy behind her ear.
She **d**id a **d**ance and sang a song,
And I stood watching all **d**ay long.

Materials

- pocket chart
- sentence strips
- letter card (*Dd*; page 79)
- picture cards (deer, daisy; page 87)
- alphabet frame (page 83)
- blank picture card template (page 83)
- old magazines and workbooks (optional)
- alphabet mini-book (pages 110–111)
- mini-book letter strips (*Dd*; pages 112–113)

Getting Ready

1. Copy the title and poem onto sentence strips (one line per sentence strip). Highlight the letter *Dd* in the initial position (as indicated above). Place the sentence strips in order in the pocket chart.

2. Photocopy and cut apart the picture cards (deer, daisy). If desired, color them and laminate for durability.

3. Place the picture cards and the letter card (in that order) in the pocket chart across the top.

4. Customize the alphabet mini-book for the letter *Dd*. (See page 5 for directions.)

Teaching With the Pocket Chart Poem

1. Point to the picture card for *deer*, and ask children what they see. Say the word *deer*, emphasizing the /d/ sound, and have children repeat it. Then ask: *What letter of the alphabet makes the /d/ sound?* Point to the uppercase and lowercase *Dd* and have children name each letter. Then ask them to identify the other picture whose name begins with the /d/ sound and the letter *d* (daisy).

2. Invite children to get ready to listen to a poem about a very special deer. As you read the poem, emphasize words that begin with the /d/ sound. Place the picture cards alongside corresponding lines to reinforce sound-letter associations. When you read the poem a second time, pause after each pair of lines. Invite volunteers to take turns using the alphabet frame to isolate each letter *d* that begins a word and represents the /d/ sound. Together, read the words aloud.

3. Ask children to think of other words that begin with the /d/ sound and the letter *d*—for example, *duck, doll, donkey, dog,* and *dolphin*. Write their suggestions on sentence strips and trim to size. Make picture cards to match children's new words (using the blank picture card template and pictures you draw or cut from old magazines or workbooks). Place the new word and picture cards in the pocket chart. Keep the pocket chart on display so that children can revisit the poem, pictures, and words over the next few days.

4. Write the letters *D* and *d* slowly on chart paper (or a whiteboard) to model their formation. Have children follow your movements by taking turns and using their finger to write each letter on a partner's back.

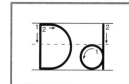

5. Give each child a copy of the alphabet mini-book. Have children use their finger to trace the letter *Dd* in the title. After completing pages 2–4 (see page 5 for directions), invite children to use the back of page 4 (or another sheet of paper) to draw a picture about the letter *Dd*. Using the poem as inspiration, they might draw the deer doing a dance. Or they might incorporate other ideas—for example, drawing the deer and a duck eating dinner together.

The Letter *Ee* (short *e*)

Eddie Elephant

Eddie **E**lephant is an **e**xcellent cook.

He g**e**ts t**e**n r**e**cipes from a sp**e**cial book.

He makes v**e**ry good **e**ggs and the b**e**st ch**e**rry pie.

His Fr**e**nch toast with j**e**lly, you simply must try!

His p**e**pper and v**e**getable soups are divine.

Everything **E**ddie creates is so fine!

Materials

- ✿ pocket chart
- ✿ sentence strips
- ✿ letter card (*Ee*; page 79)
- ✿ picture cards (elephant, 10, eggs; pages 87–88)
- ✿ alphabet frame (page 83)
- ✿ blank picture card template (page 83)
- ✿ old magazines and workbooks (optional)
- ✿ alphabet mini-book (pages 110–111)
- ✿ mini-book letter strips (*Ee*; pages 112–113)

Getting Ready

1. Copy the title and poem onto sentence strips (one line per sentence strip). Highlight the letter *Ee* in the initial and medial position (as indicated above). Place the sentence strips in order in the pocket chart.

2. Photocopy and cut apart the picture cards (elephant, 10, eggs). If desired, color them and laminate for durability.

3. Place the picture cards and the letter card (in that order) in the pocket chart across the top.

4. Customize the alphabet mini-book for the letter *Ee*. (See page 5 for directions.)

Teaching With the Pocket Chart Poem

1. Begin by pointing to the picture card for *elephant*; ask children what they see. Say the word *elephant*, emphasizing the /e/ sound at the beginning of the word. Have children repeat it. Ask: *What letter of the alphabet makes the /e/ sound at the beginning of the word* elephant? Point to the uppercase and lowercase *Ee* and have children name each letter. Then have them look at the other picture cards and name something else that begins with the /e/ sound and the letter *e* (eggs).

2. Explain: *Sometimes we hear the /e/ sound in the middle of a word.* Point to the numeral 10 and have children say the word. Ask: *What sound do you hear in the middle of the word* ten? (/e/) *What letter makes the /e/ sound?* (e)

3. Tell children to get ready to listen to a poem about an elephant named Eddie that likes to cook. As you read the poem, emphasize words that have an initial or a medial /e/ sound. Place the picture cards alongside corresponding lines to reinforce sound-letter associations. When you read the poem a second time, pause after each pair of lines. Invite volunteers to take turns using the alphabet frame to isolate each letter *e* that represents the /e/ sound. Together, read the words aloud.

4. Ask children to think of other words that are like *elephant* and begin with the /e/ sound and the letter *e*, such as *envelope, elf,* and *end*. Repeat for words that are like *ten*, and have the /e/ sound and the letter *e* in the middle (such as *bed* and *pet*). Make picture cards to match children's new words (using the blank picture card template and pictures you draw or cut from old magazines or workbooks). Place the new word and picture cards in the pocket chart. Keep the pocket chart on display so that children can enjoy reading the poem and the words over the next few days.

5. Write the letters *E* and *e* slowly on chart paper (or a whiteboard) to model their formation. Have children follow your movements by using their finger to write each letter on their palm.

6. Give each child a copy of the alphabet mini-book. Have children use their finger to trace the letter *Ee* in the title. After completing pages 2–4 (see page 5 for directions), invite children to use the back of page 4 (or another sheet of paper) to draw a picture of Eddie Elephant making a cherry pie, or French toast and jelly.

The Letter **Ee** (long e)

Sweet Dreams

J**ea**n went to sl**ee**p,

And had a sw**ee**t dr**ea**m.

She dr**ea**med of thr**ee** scoops of vanilla ice cr**ea**m!

She dr**ea**med about hon**ey**

That comes from the b**ee**s.

She dr**ea**med about p**ea**ches that grow on gr**ee**n tr**ee**s.

When J**ea**n woke up, she said to her dad,

"That's the best dr**ea**m I've ever had!"

Materials

🌀 pocket chart

🌀 sentence strips

🌀 letter card (*Ee*; page 79)

🌀 picture cards (sleep, 3, ice cream, bees, trees; pages 88–89)

🌀 blank picture card template (page 83)

🌀 old magazines and workbooks (optional)

🌀 alphabet mini-book (pages 110–111)

🌀 mini-book letter strips (*Ee*; pages 112–113)

Getting Ready

1. Copy the title and poem onto sentence strips (one line per sentence strip). Highlight the letters that make the long *e* sound (as indicated above). Place the sentence strips in order in the pocket chart.

2. Photocopy and cut apart the picture cards (sleep, 3, ice cream, bees, trees). If desired, color them and laminate for durability.

3. Place the picture cards and the letter card (in that order) in the pocket chart across the top.

4. Customize the alphabet mini-book for the letter *Ee*. (See page 5 for directions.)

Teaching With the Pocket Chart Poem

1. Begin by pointing to the picture card for *sleep*; ask children to say the name of the picture. Say the word *sleep* again, emphasizing the /ē/ sound; have children repeat it. Then write the word *sleep* on chart paper (or a whiteboard), and point out that the letters *ee* make the /ē/ sound, which is the long-*e* sound. Continue in the same way with the picture cards for *3, bees, peaches,* and *trees.* Guide children to recognize that the letters *ea* (as in *peaches*) can also make the /ē/ sound.

2. Invite children to get ready to listen to a poem about someone who has a sweet dream. As you read the poem and track the print, emphasize the words that have a long-*e* sound. Place the picture cards alongside corresponding lines to reinforce sound-letter associations. When you read the poem a second time, pause after each pair of lines. Invite volunteers to take turns pointing to each word that contains the long-*e* sound. Together, read these words aloud. Be sure to point out that in the word *She*, the letter *e* makes the long-*e* sound, and in the word *honey*, the letters *ey* make the long-*e* sound.

3. Ask children to think of other words with the long-*e* sound—for example, *queen, seal, feet, team, me,* and *key.* Write their suggestions on sentence strips and trim to size. Point out the letter or letters in each word that form the long-*e* sound (*ee, ea, e,* and *ey*). Make picture cards to match children's new words (using the blank picture card template and pictures you draw or cut from old magazines or workbooks). Place the new word and picture cards in the pocket chart. Keep the pocket chart on display so that children can enjoy revisiting the poem, pictures, and words over the next few days.

4. Write the letters *E* and *e* slowly on chart paper (or a whiteboard) to model their formation. Have children follow your movements by using their finger to write each letter on their palm.

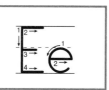

5. Give each child a copy of the alphabet mini-book. Have children use their finger to trace the letter *Ee* in the title. After completing pages 2–4 (see page 5 for directions), invite children to use the back of page 4 (or another sheet of paper) to draw a picture of Jean's sweet dream (or a dream of their own).

The Letter *Ff*

One Fine Fox

In the **f**orest there lived a **f**ox
Who was a **f**unny chatterbox!
He talked so **f**ast my head would spin.
Sometimes I couldn't **f**ollow him!
"Slow down, **f**ine **f**ellow," I would say.
"There's lots of time to talk all day!"

Materials

❀ pocket chart

❀ sentence strips

❀ letter card (*Ff*; page 79)

❀ picture cards (forest, fox; pages 89–90)

❀ alphabet frame (page 83)

❀ blank picture card template (page 83)

❀ old magazines and workbooks (optional)

❀ alphabet mini-book (pages 110–111)

❀ mini-book letter strips (*Ff*; pages 112–113)

Getting Ready

1. Copy the title and poem onto sentence strips (one line per sentence strip). Highlight the letter *Ff* in the initial position (as indicated above). Place the sentence strips in order in the pocket chart.

2. Photocopy and cut apart the picture cards (forest, fox). If desired, color them and laminate for durability.

3. Place the picture cards and the letter card (in that order) in the pocket chart across the top.

4. Customize the alphabet mini-book for the letter *Ff*. (See page 5 for directions.)

Teaching With the Pocket Chart Poem

1. Point to the picture card for *fox*, and ask children what they see. Say the word *fox*, emphasizing the /f/ sound; have children repeat it. Then ask: *What letter of the alphabet makes the /f/ sound?* Point to the uppercase and lowercase *Ff* and have children name each letter. Then have them identify the other picture whose name begins with the /f/ sound and the letter *f* (forest).

2. Invite children to get ready to listen to a poem about a fox that talked very fast. As you read the poem, emphasize the words that begin with the /f/ sound. Place the picture cards alongside corresponding lines to reinforce sound-letter associations. When you read the poem a second time, pause after each pair of lines. Invite volunteers to take turns using the alphabet frame to isolate each letter *f* that begins a word and represents the /f/ sound. Together, read these words aloud.

3. Ask children to think of other words that begin with the /f/ sound and the letter *f*—for example, *fan, farm, fire, foot,* and *fish*. Write their suggestions on sentence strips, and trim to size. Make picture cards to match children's new words (using the blank picture card template and pictures you draw or cut from old magazines or workbooks). Place the new word and picture cards in the pocket chart. Keep the pocket chart on display, and encourage children to revisit the poem, pictures, and words over the next few days.

4. Write the letters *F* and *f* slowly on chart paper (or a whiteboard) to model their formation. Have children follow your movements, using their finger to write the letters in the air or on the palms of their hands.

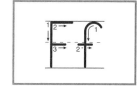

5. Give each child a copy of the alphabet mini-book. Have children use their finger to trace the letter *Ff* in the title. After completing pages 2–4 (see page 5 for directions), invite children to use the back of page 4 (or another sheet of paper) to draw a picture of the fox doing something that represents the letter *Ff*, such as feeding four fish or eating food with a fork.

The Letter Gg

A Gift for Goat

Goose **g**ave a special **g**ift to **G**oat.
It wasn't a **g**ame or a new winter coat.
It was a **g**orgeous **g**uitar that **G**oat could play,
And have a **g**ood time as he sings all day!

Materials

- pocket chart
- sentence strips
- letter card (*Gg*; page 80)
- picture cards (goose, gift, goat, guitar; pages 90–91)
- alphabet frame (page 83)
- blank picture card template (page 83)
- old magazines and workbooks (optional)
- alphabet mini-book (pages 110–111)
- mini-book letter strips (*Gg*; pages 112, 114)

Getting Ready

1. Copy the title and poem onto sentence strips (one line per sentence strip). Highlight the letter G*g* in the initial position (as indicated above). Place the sentence strips in order in the pocket chart.

2. Photocopy and cut apart the picture cards (goose, gift, goat, guitar). If desired, color them and laminate for durability.

3. Place the picture cards and the letter card (in that order) in the pocket chart across the top.

4. Customize the alphabet mini-book for the letter G*g*. (See page 5 for directions.)

Teaching With the Pocket Chart Poem

1. Point to the picture card for *goose*, and ask children what they see. Say the word *goose*, emphasizing the /g/ sound; have children repeat it. Then ask: *What letter of the alphabet makes the /g/ sound?* Point to the uppercase and lowercase *Gg* and have children name each letter. Then have them identify the other pictures whose names begin with the /g/ sound and the letter *g* (gift, goat, guitar).

2. Invite children to get ready to listen to a poem about a goose and a goat. As you read the poem, emphasize the words that begin with the /g/ sound. Place the picture cards alongside corresponding lines to reinforce sound-letter associations. When you read the poem a second time, pause after each pair of lines. Invite volunteers to take turns using the alphabet frame to isolate each letter *g* that begins a word and represents the /g/ sound. Together, read these words aloud.

3. Ask children to think of other words that begin with the /g/ sound and the letter *g*—for example, *girl, garden, goldfish,* and *gate*. Write their suggestions on sentence strips, and trim to size. Make picture cards to match children's new words (using the blank picture card template and pictures you draw or cut from old magazines or workbooks). Place the new word and picture cards in the pocket chart. Keep the pocket chart on display, and encourage children to revisit the poem, pictures, and words over the next few days.

4. Write the letters *G* and *g* slowly on chart paper (or a whiteboard) to model their formation. Have children follow your movements by taking turns and using their finger to write each letter on a partner's back.

5. Give each child a copy of the alphabet mini-book. Have children use their finger to trace the letter *Gg* in the title. After completing pages 2–4 (see page 5 for directions), invite children to use the back of page 4 (or another sheet of paper) to draw a picture of the goose and goat playing a game together.

The Letter *Hh*

A Happy Hare

One day I met a **h**appy **h**are.
That liked to **h**op from **h**ere to there.
On **h**is **h**armonica **h**e played a tune,
And **h**opped around all afternoon!

Materials

* pocket chart
* sentence strips
* letter card (*Hh*; page 80)
* picture cards (hare, harmonica; page 91)
* alphabet frame (page 83)
* blank picture card template (page 83)
* old magazines and workbooks (optional)
* alphabet mini-book (pages 110–111)
* mini-book letter strips (*Hh*; pages 112, 114)

Getting Ready

1. Copy the title and poem onto sentence strips (one line per sentence strip). Highlight the letter *Hh* in the initial position (as indicated above). Place the sentence strips in order in the pocket chart.

2. Photocopy and cut apart the picture cards (hare, harmonica). If desired, color them and laminate for durability.

3. Place the picture cards and the letter card (in that order) in the pocket chart across the top.

4. Customize the alphabet mini-book for the letter *Hh*. (See page 5 for directions.)

Teaching With the Pocket Chart Poem

1. Point to the picture card for *hare*, and ask children what they see. Invite children to tell what they know about hares. Explain that a hare looks very much like a rabbit but is larger. Say the word *hare*, emphasizing the /h/ sound; have children repeat it. Then ask: *What letter of the alphabet makes the /h/ sound?* Point to the uppercase and lowercase *Hh* and have children name each letter. Invite them to tell what the other picture shows (harmonica). Point out that this word also begins with the /h/ sound and the letter *h*.

2. Invite children to get ready to listen to a poem about a happy hare. As you read the poem, emphasize the words that begin with the /h/ sound. Place the picture cards alongside corresponding lines to reinforce sound-letter associations. When you read the poem a second time, pause after each pair of lines. Invite volunteers to take turns using the alphabet frame to isolate each letter *h* that begins a word and represents the /h/ sound. Together, read these words aloud.

3. Ask children to think of other words that begin with the /h/ sound and the letter *h*—for example, *horse, hat, hand, heart,* and *house*. Write their suggestions on sentence strips, and trim to size. Make picture cards to match children's new words (using the blank picture card template and pictures you draw or cut from old magazines or workbooks). Place the new word and picture cards in the pocket chart. Keep the pocket chart on display, and encourage children to revisit the poem, pictures, and words over the next few days.

4. Write the letters *H* and *h* slowly on chart paper (or a whiteboard) to model their formation. Have children follow your movements by using their finger to write each letter in the air.

5. Give each child a copy of the alphabet mini-book. Have children use their finger to trace the letter *Hh* in the title. After completing pages 2–4 (see page 5 for directions), invite children to use the back of page 4 (or another sheet of paper) to draw a picture of the happy hare hopping down a hill. Or they might draw the hare in another setting with objects that represent the letter *Hh*, such as in a house with a hat hanging on a hook.

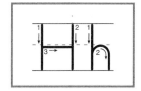

The Letter *Ii* (short *i*)

Six Little Inchworms

Six little inchworms walk up a hill,

Inch by inch,

They don't sit still.

At the top of the hill, they nibble and sip,

They're happy to finish their very long trip!

Materials

🌸 pocket chart

🌸 sentence strips

🌸 letter card (*Ii*; page 80)

🌸 picture cards
   (6, inchworms, hill,
   inch; pages 91–92)

🌸 alphabet frame (page 83)

🌸 blank picture card
   template (page 83)

🌸 old magazines and
   workbooks (optional)

🌸 alphabet mini-book
   (pages 110–111)

🌸 mini-book letter strips
   (*Ii*; pages 112, 114)

Getting Ready

1. Copy the title and poem onto sentence strips (one line per sentence strip). Highlight the letter *Ii* in the initial and medial position (as indicated above). Place the sentence strips in order in the pocket chart.

2. Photocopy and cut apart the picture cards (6, inchworms, hill, inch). If desired, color them and laminate for durability.

3. Place the picture cards and the letter card (in that order) in the pocket chart across the top.

4. Customize the alphabet mini-book for the letter *Ii*. (See page 5 for directions.)

32 *The Big Book of Pocket Chart Poems: ABCs & 123s*

Teaching With the Pocket Chart Poem

1. Begin by pointing to the picture card for *inchworms*, and ask children what they see. Invite children to tell what they know about inchworms—for example, they're a type of insect and are sometimes called measuring worms. Say the word *inchworms*, emphasizing the /i/ sound, and have children repeat. Then ask: *What letter of the alphabet makes the /i/ sound?* Point to the uppercase and lowercase *Ii* and have children name each letter. Then have them find another picture card whose name begins with the /i/ sound and the letter *i* (inch).

2. Explain: *Sometimes we hear the /i/ sound in the middle of a word.* Point to the picture cards for *six* and *hill* and have children say the words. Ask: *What sound do you hear in the middle of the words* six *and* hill? (/i/) *What letter makes the /i/ sound?* (i)

3. Tell children that you're going to share a poem about six inchworms that climb a hill. As you read the poem, emphasize words that have an initial or a medial /i/ sound. Place the picture cards alongside corresponding lines to reinforce sound-letter associations. When you read the poem a second time, pause after each pair of lines. Invite volunteers to take turns using the alphabet frame to isolate each letter *i* that represents the /i/ sound. Together, read these words aloud.

4. Ask children to think of words that are like *inchworm* and begin with the /i/ sound and the letter *i*, such as *igloo*, *ink*, and *iguana*. Repeat for words that are like *six* and have the /i/ sound and the letter *i* in the middle, such as *fish*, *pig*, and *dish*. Write their suggestions on sentence strips, and trim to size. Make picture cards to match the new words (using the blank picture card template and pictures you draw or cut from old magazines or workbooks). Place the new cards in the pocket chart, and keep it on display for children to revisit.

5. Write the letters *I* and *i* slowly on chart paper (or a whiteboard) to model their formation. Have children follow your movements using their finger to write each letter on their palm.

6. Give each child a copy of the alphabet mini-book. Have children use their finger to trace the letter *Ii* in the title. After completing pages 2–4 (see page 5 for directions), invite children to use the back of page 4 (or another sheet of paper) to draw a picture of the six inchworms. Encourage children to incorporate in their picture objects whose names begin with the /i/ sound, such as six inchworms inching their way up a stick.

The Letter *Ii* (long *i*)

What I Like

I l**i**k**e** to read,
I l**i**k**e** to wr**i**t**e**,
I l**i**k**e** to run and fly a k**i**t**e**.
I l**i**k**e** to walk,
I l**i**k**e** to h**i**k**e**,
I l**i**k**e** to r**i**d**e** my brand-new b**i**k**e**.
I l**i**k**e** to swim,
I l**i**k**e** to d**i**v**e**,
One day, **I** know **I**'d l**i**k**e** to drive!

Materials

- pocket chart
- sentence strips
- letter card (*Ii*; page 80)
- picture cards (kite, bike, dive; pages 92–93)
- blank picture card template (page 83)
- old magazines and workbooks (optional)
- alphabet mini-book (pages 110–111)
- mini-book letter strips (*Ii*; pages 112, 114)

Getting Ready

1. Copy the title and poem onto sentence strips (one line per sentence strip). Highlight the letters that form the long-*i* sound (as indicated above). Place the sentence strips in order in the pocket chart.

2. Photocopy and cut apart the picture cards (kite, bike, dive). If desired, color them and laminate for durability.

3. Place the picture cards and the letter card (in that order) in the pocket chart across the top.

4. Customize the alphabet mini-book for the letter *Ii*. (See page 5 for directions.)

Teaching With the Pocket Chart Poem

1. Begin by pointing to the picture card for *kite*, and asking children to say the name of the picture. Say the word *kite* again, emphasizing the /ī/ sound; have children repeat it. Then write the word *kite* on chart paper (or a whiteboard), and point out that the letters *i_e* make the /ī/ sound, which is the long-*i* sound. Continue in the same way with the picture cards for *bike* and *dive*.

2. Invite children to get ready to listen to a poem that tells about all the things someone likes to do. As you read the poem and track the print, emphasize the words that have a long-*i* sound. Place the picture cards alongside corresponding lines to reinforce sound-letter associations. When you read the poem a second time, pause after each line or pair of lines. Call on children to come to the chart to point to and say each word that has a long-*i* sound. Then read each word aloud with the group. Be sure to point out that in the words *fly* and *my*, the letter *y* makes the long-*i* sound.

3. Ask children to think of other words with the long-*i* sound—for example, *hide*, *dime*, *life*, *smile*, *side*, and *try*. Write their suggestions on sentence strips, and trim to size. Point out the letter or letters in each word that form the long-*i* sound (*i_e* and *y*). Make picture cards to match children's new words (using the blank picture card template and pictures you draw or cut from old magazines or workbooks). Place the new word and picture cards in the pocket chart. Keep the pocket chart on display, and encourage children to revisit the poem, pictures, and words over the next few days.

4. Write the letters *I* and *i* slowly on chart paper (or a whiteboard) to model their formation. Have children follow your movements by taking turns and using their finger to write each letter on their palm.

5. Give each child a copy of the alphabet mini-book. Have children use their finger to trace the letter *Ii* in the title. After completing pages 2–4 (see page 5 for directions), invite children to use the back of page 4 (or another sheet of paper) to draw a picture of themselves doing something they like from the poem (such as fly a kite or ride a bike).

The Letter *Jj*

J Is for Juggler

A **j**uggler likes to **j**uggle,
And a **j**aguar likes to run,
A **j**ack-o'-lantern likes to smile
As though it's having fun!
A **j**ogger likes to **j**og,
And **j**elly likes to **j**iggle,
And me, I like to tell a **j**oke
That makes my best friend giggle!

Materials

* pocket chart
* sentence strips
* letter card (*Jj*; page 80)
* picture cards (juggler, jaguar, jack-o'-lantern, jelly; pages 93–94)
* alphabet frame (page 83)
* blank picture card template (page 83)
* old magazines and workbooks (optional)
* alphabet mini-book (pages 110–111)
* mini-book letter strips (*Jj*; pages 112, 114)

Getting Ready

1. Copy the title and poem onto sentence strips (one line per sentence strip). Highlight the letter *Jj* in the initial position (as indicated above). Place the sentence strips in order in the pocket chart.

2. Photocopy and cut apart the picture cards (juggler, jaguar, jack-o'-lantern, jelly). If desired, color them and laminate for durability.

3. Place the picture cards and the letter card (in that order) in the pocket chart across the top.

4. Customize the alphabet mini-book for the letter *Jj*. (See page 5 for directions.)

Teaching With the Pocket Chart Poem

1. Begin by pointing to the picture card for *juggler*. Ask children what they see. Say the word *juggler*, emphasizing the /j/ sound, and have children repeat it. Then ask: *What letter of the alphabet makes the /j/ sound?* Point to the uppercase and lowercase *Jj* and have children name each letter. Then have them identify the other pictures whose names begin with the /j/ sound and the letter *j* (jaguar, jack-o'-lantern, jelly).

2. Ask children what a juggler likes to do (juggle balls or other things). Explain that children will be listening to a poem that describes what different people, animals, and things like to do. As you read the poem, emphasize the words that begin with the /j/ sound. Place the picture cards alongside corresponding lines to reinforce sound-letter associations. When you read the poem a second time, pause after each pair of lines. Invite volunteers to take turns using the alphabet frame to isolate each letter *j* that begins a word and represents the /j/ sound. Together, read these words aloud.

3. Ask children to think of other words that begin with the /j/ sound and the letter *j*—for example, *jump*, *jam*, *juice*, *jungle*, and *jet*. Write their suggestions on sentence strips, and trim to size. Make picture cards to match children's new words (using the blank picture card template and pictures you draw or cut from old magazines or workbooks). Place the new word and picture cards in the pocket chart. Keep the pocket chart on display, and encourage children to revisit the poem, pictures, and words over the next few days.

4. Write the letters *J* and *j* slowly on chart paper (or a whiteboard) to model their formation. Have children follow your movements by taking turns using their finger to write each letter on a partner's back.

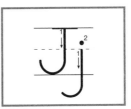

5. Give each child a copy of the alphabet mini-book. Have children use their finger to trace the letter *Jj* in the title. After completing pages 2–4 (see page 5 for directions), invite children to use the back of page 4 (or another sheet of paper) to draw a picture about the letter *Jj*. They might draw a picture to go with the poem, or come up with a new idea—for example, a picture of them jumping rope with a friend.

The Letter *Kk*

Two Little Kittens

I have two little **k**ittens.
I **k**iss them every day.
I **k**eep my **k**ittens happy.
I like to watch them play.
I'm always **k**ind and gentle
In everything I do.
I love my little **k**ittens.
My **k**ittens love me, too!

Materials

- pocket chart
- sentence strips
- letter card (*Kk*; page 80)
- picture card (kittens; page 94)
- alphabet frame (page 83)
- blank picture card template (page 83)
- old magazines and workbooks (optional)
- alphabet mini-book (pages 110–111)
- mini-book letter strips (*Kk*; pages 112, 114)

Getting Ready

1. Copy the title and poem onto sentence strips (one line per sentence strip). Highlight the letter *Kk* in the initial position (as indicated above). Place the sentence strips in order in the pocket chart.

2. Photocopy and cut apart the picture card (kittens). If desired, color it and laminate for durability.

3. Place the picture card and the letter card (in that order) in the pocket chart across the top.

4. Customize the alphabet mini-book for the letter *Kk*. (See page 5 for directions.)

Teaching With the Pocket Chart Poem

1. Point to the picture card for *kittens*, and ask children what they see. Say the word *kittens*, emphasizing the /k/ sound, and have children repeat it. Then ask: *What letter of the alphabet makes the /k/ sound?* (If children know that the letter *c* also makes the /k/ sound, explain that both *c* and *k* make the /k/ sound.) Point to the uppercase and lowercase *Kk* and have children name each letter.

2. Invite children to get ready to listen to a poem about a child who has two kittens. As you read the poem, emphasize the words that begin with the /k/ sound. Place the picture card alongside a corresponding line to reinforce sound-letter associations. When you read the poem a second time, pause after each pair of lines. Invite volunteers to take turns using the alphabet frame to isolate each letter *k* that begins a word and represents the /k/ sound. Together, read these words aloud.

3. Invite children to think of other words that begin with the /k/ sound and the letter *k*— for example, *key, kangaroo, king, koala,* and *kindergarten*. Write their suggestions on sentence strips, and trim to size. Make picture cards to match children's new words (using the blank picture card template and pictures you draw or cut from old magazines or workbooks). Place the new word and picture cards in the pocket chart. Keep the pocket chart on display, and encourage children to revisit the poem, pictures, and words over the next few days.

4. Write the letters *K* and *k* slowly on chart paper (or a whiteboard) to model their formation. Have children follow your movements, writing each letter in the air.

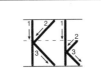

5. Give each child a copy of the alphabet mini-book. Have children use their finger to trace the letter *Kk* in the title. After completing pages 2–4 (see page 5 for directions), invite children to use the back of page 4 (or another sheet of paper) to draw a picture of the two kittens eating their food in the kitchen.

The Letter *Ll*

Ladybug and Lion

One day as a **l**ion was starting to doze,
A **l**ittle red **l**adybug fell on his nose!
"I'm sorry to wake you, dear **l**ion," she said.
"But I fell off a **l**eaf to **l**and right on your head!"
The **l**ion **l**aughed **l**oudly and said, "That's okay.
You **l**ook very nice and I'd **l**ike you to stay!"

Materials

- pocket chart
- sentence strips
- letter card (*Ll*; page 80)
- picture cards (lion, ladybug, leaf; pages 94–95)
- alphabet frame (page 83)
- blank picture card template (page 83)
- old magazines and workbooks (optional)
- alphabet mini-book (pages 110–111)
- mini-book letter strips (*Ll*; pages 112, 115)

Getting Ready

1. Copy the title and poem onto sentence strips (one line per sentence strip). Highlight the letter *Ll* in the initial position (as indicated above). Place the sentence strips in order in the pocket chart.

2. Photocopy and cut apart the picture cards (lion, ladybug, leaf). If desired, color them and laminate for durability.

3. Place the picture cards and the letter card (in that order) in the pocket chart across the top.

4. Customize the alphabet mini-book for the letter *Ll*. (See page 5 for directions.)

Teaching With the Pocket Chart Poem

1. Begin by pointing to the picture card for *lion*, and ask children what they see. Say the word *lion*, emphasizing the /l/ sound; have children repeat it. Ask: *What letter of the alphabet makes the /l/ sound?* Point to the uppercase and lowercase *Ll* and have children name each letter. Ask them to identify the other pictures whose names begin with the /l/ sound and the letter *l* (ladybug, leaf).

2. Invite children to get ready to listen to a poem about a lion and a ladybug. As you read the poem, emphasize those words that begin with the /l/ sound. Place the picture cards alongside corresponding lines to reinforce sound-letter associations. When you read the poem a second time, pause after each pair of lines. Invite volunteers to take turns using the alphabet frame to isolate each letter *l* that begins a word and represents the /l/ sound. Together, read these words aloud.

3. Ask children to think of other words that begin with the /l/ sound and the letter *l*—for example, *lake, leg, ladder, letter,* and *lunchbox*. Write their suggestions on sentence strips, and trim to size. Make picture cards to match children's new words (using the blank picture card template and pictures you draw or cut from old magazines or workbooks). Place the new word and picture cards in the pocket chart. Keep the pocket chart on display, and encourage children to revisit the poem, pictures, and words over the next few days.

4. Write the letters *L* and *l* slowly on chart paper (or a whiteboard) to model their formation. Have children follow your movements by using their finger to write each letter on their palm.

5. Give each child a copy of the alphabet mini-book. Have children use their finger to trace the letter *Ll* in the title. After completing pages 2–4 (see page 5 for directions), invite children to use the back of page 4 (or another sheet of paper) to draw a picture that shows that the lion and the ladybug like each other.

The Letter *Mm*

Monkey at the Market

On a summer **m**orning that was bright and sunny,

A **m**onkey went to **m**arket with all of his **m**oney.

He bought **m**any **m**arvelous things to eat,

Like **m**angos and **m**ushrooms, **m**elons and **m**eat.

He got **m**uffins and **m**ilk and **m**arshmallows galore,

And kept shopping until he had **m**oney no **m**ore!

Materials

❁ pocket chart

❁ sentence strips

❁ letter card (*Mm*; page 81)

❁ picture cards (monkey, money, mushrooms, muffins, milk, marshmallows; pages 95–96)

❁ alphabet frame (page 83)

❁ blank picture card template (page 83)

❁ old magazines and workbooks (optional)

❁ alphabet mini-book (pages 110–111)

❁ mini-book letter strips (*Mm*; pages 112, 115)

Getting Ready

1. Copy the title and poem onto sentence strips (one line per sentence strip). Highlight the letter *Mm* in the initial position (as indicated above). Place the sentence strips in order in the pocket chart.

2. Photocopy and cut apart the picture cards (monkey, money, mushrooms, muffins, milk, marshmallows). If desired, color them and laminate for durability.

3. Place the picture cards and the letter card (in that order) in the pocket chart across the top.

4. Customize the alphabet mini-book for the letter *Mm*. (See page 5 for directions.)

Teaching With the Pocket Chart Poem

1. Point to the picture card for *monkey*, and ask children what they see. Say the word *monkey*, emphasizing the /m/ sound; have children repeat it. Then ask: *What letter of the alphabet makes the /m/ sound?* Point to the uppercase and lowercase M*m* and have children name each letter. Ask them to identify the names of the other pictures that begin with the /m/ sound and the letter *m* (money, mushrooms, muffins, milk, marshmallows).

2. Invite children to get ready to listen to a poem about a monkey that went to a market to buy food. As you read the poem, emphasize the words that begin with the /m/ sound. Place the picture cards alongside corresponding lines to reinforce sound-letter associations. When you read the poem a second time, pause after each pair of lines. Invite volunteers to take turns using the alphabet frame to isolate each letter *m* that begins a word and represents the /m/ sound. Together, read these words aloud.

3. Invite children to think of other words that begin with the /m/ sound and the letter *m*—for example, *mask, moon, mailbox, mitten,* and *map*. Write their suggestions on sentence strips, and trim to size. Make picture cards to match children's new words (using the blank picture card template and pictures you draw or cut from old magazines or workbooks). Place the new word and picture cards in the pocket chart. Keep the pocket chart on display, and encourage children to revisit the poem, pictures, and words over the next few days.

4. Write the letters M and *m* slowly on chart paper (or a whiteboard) to model their formation. Have children follow your movements by writing each letter in the air.

5. Give each child a copy of the alphabet mini-book. Have children use their finger to trace the letter M*m* in the title. After completing pages 2–4 (see page 5 for directions), invite children to use the back of page 4 (or another sheet of paper) to draw a picture of the monkey at home, drinking a glass of milk and eating a muffin. Or children might like to draw the monkey in another activity that represents the letter M*m*, such as playing marbles or doing math!

The Letter *Nn*

Never Ever

Have you ever eaten **n**oodles or **n**uts at **n**oon?

Or **n**ibbled on berries while you sang a tune?

I **n**ever have. Have you?

Have you ever been messy when you should have been **n**eat?

Or acted kind of **n**aughty when you should have been sweet?

No, I **n**ever have. Have you?

Have you ever lost a **n**ickel or even a dime?

Or tried to make up a **n**onsense rhyme?

I **n**ever, ever have. How about you?

Materials

- pocket chart
- sentence strips
- letter card (*Nn*; page 81)
- picture cards (noodles, nuts, noon, nickel; page 97)
- alphabet frame (page 83)
- blank picture card template (page 83)
- old magazines and workbooks (optional)
- alphabet mini-book (pages 110–111)
- mini-book letter strips (*Nn*; pages 112, 115)

Getting Ready

1. Copy the title and poem onto sentence strips (one line per sentence strip). Highlight the letter *Nn* in the initial position (as indicated above). Place the sentence strips in order in the pocket chart.

2. Photocopy and cut apart the picture cards (noodles, nuts, noon, nickel). If desired, color them and laminate for durability.

3. Place the picture cards and the letter card (in that order) in the pocket chart across the top.

4. Customize the alphabet mini-book for the letter *Nn*. (See page 5 for directions.)

Teaching With the Pocket Chart Poem

1. Point to the picture card for *noodles*, and ask children what they see. Say the word *noodles*, emphasizing the /n/ sound, and have children repeat it. Then ask: *What letter of the alphabet makes the /n/ sound?* Point to the uppercase and lowercase *Nn* and have children name each letter. Ask them to identify the names of the other pictures that begin with the /n/ sound and the letter *n* (nuts, noon, nickel).

2. Invite children to get ready to listen to a poem that asks questions about noodles, nuts, and lots of other things. As you read the poem, emphasize words that begin with the /n/ sound. Place the picture cards alongside corresponding lines to reinforce sound-letter associations. When you read the poem a second time, pause after each pair of lines. Invite volunteers to take turns using the alphabet frame to isolate each letter *n* that begins a word and represents the /n/ sound. Together, read these words aloud.

3. Ask children to think of other words that begin with the /n/ sound and the letter *n*—for example, *nine*, *necklace*, *nest*, *napkin*, and *nose*. Write their suggestions on sentence strips, and trim to size. Make picture cards to match children's new words (using the blank picture card template and pictures you draw or cut from old magazines or workbooks). Place the new word and picture cards in the pocket chart. Keep the pocket chart on display, and encourage children to revisit the poem, pictures, and words over the next few days.

4. Write the letters *N* and *n* slowly on chart paper (or a whiteboard) to model their formation. Have children follow your movements by taking turns and using their finger to write each letter on a partner's back.

5. Give each child a copy of the alphabet mini-book. Have children use their finger to trace the letter *Nn* in the title. After completing pages 2–4 (see page 5 for directions), invite children to use the back of page 4 (or another sheet of paper) to draw a picture of themselves eating a bowl of noodles at night. Encourage children to include other details in their pictures that show things with names that start with the letter *Nn*.

The Letter Oo (short o)

Ostrich and Ox

Ostrich and **O**x go sh**o**pping
For l**o**ts of things they need.
After a while, their sh**o**pping bags
Are very full indeed!
They get cl**o**cks and m**o**ps and p**o**pcorn,
And some fancy flowerp**o**ts.
They get d**o**lls and l**o**gs and **o**lives,
And blue s**o**cks with polka d**o**ts!

Materials

- pocket chart
- sentence strips
- letter card (*Oo*; page 81)
- picture cards (ostrich, ox, shopping bags, clocks, mops, popcorn, dolls, logs, socks; pages 98–100)
- alphabet frame (page 83)
- blank picture card template (page 83)
- old magazines and workbooks (optional)
- alphabet mini-book (pages 110–111)
- mini-book letter strips (*Oo*; pages 112, 115)

Getting Ready

1. Copy the title and poem onto sentence strips (one line per sentence strip). Highlight the letter *Oo* in the initial and medial position (as indicated above). Place the sentence strips in order in the pocket chart.

2. Photocopy and cut apart the picture cards (ostrich, ox, shopping bags, clocks, mops, popcorn, dolls, logs, socks). If desired, color them and laminate for durability.

3. Place the picture cards and the letter card (in that order) in the pocket chart across the top.

4. Customize the alphabet mini-book for the letter *Oo*. (See page 5 for directions.)

Teaching With the Pocket Chart Poem

1. Begin by pointing to the picture card for *ostrich*, and ask children what they see. Say the word *ostrich*, emphasizing the /o/ sound; have children repeat it. Then ask: *What letter of the alphabet makes the /o/ sound?* Point to the uppercase and lowercase *Oo* and have children name each letter. Ask them to find another picture card whose name begin with the /o/ sound and the letter *o* (ox).

2. Explain: *Sometimes the /o/ sound comes in the middle of a word.* Point to the picture card for *mops*, and have children say the word. Ask: *What sound do you hear in the middle of the word* mops? (/o/) *What letter makes the /o/ sound?* (o) Ask children to find other picture cards whose names have the /o/ sound in the middle (shopping bags, clocks, popcorn, dolls, logs, socks).

3. Tell children to get ready to listen to a poem about an ostrich and an ox that go shopping. As you read the poem, emphasize words that have an initial or a medial /o/ sound. Place the picture cards alongside corresponding lines to reinforce sound-letter associations. When you read the poem a second time, pause after each pair of lines. Invite volunteers to take turns using the alphabet frame to isolate each letter *o* that represents the /o/ sound. Together, read these words aloud.

4. Ask children to think of words that are like *ostrich* and begin with the /o/ sound and the letter *o*—for example, *octopus*, *otter*, and *October*. Repeat for words that are like *mops* and have the /o/ sound and the letter *o* in the middle, such as *rock*, *stop*, and *hot*. Write their suggestions on sentence strips, and trim to size. Make picture cards to match the new words (using the blank picture card template and pictures you draw or cut from old magazines or workbooks). Place the new word and picture cards in the pocket chart. Keep the pocket chart on display, and encourage children to revisit it over the next few days.

5. Write the letters O and o slowly on chart paper (or a whiteboard) to model their formation. Have children follow your movements, writing the letters in the air.

6. Give each child a copy of the alphabet mini-book. Have children use their finger to trace the letter *Oo* in the title. After completing pages 2–4 (see page 5 for directions), invite children to use the back of page 4 (or another sheet of paper) to draw a picture of the ostrich and ox wearing blue socks with polka dots. Children might like to go further, adding other items to their pictures that represent the letter *Oo*, such as an octopus and an otter.

The Letter Oo (long o)

Snowy Day

I w**o**ke up this morning, and what do you kn**ow**,

The r**oa**d was covered with soft white sn**ow**.

I picked up the ph**o**ne and called my friend J**oe**.

Then I put on my c**oa**t and out I did g**o**.

We built a sn**ow**man and gave him a n**o**se,

And we played in the sn**ow** till our t**oe**s alm**o**st fr**oze**.

Then I went h**o**me, and what did I do?

I wr**o**te this p**o**em about sn**ow** just for you!

Materials

- pocket chart
- sentence strips
- letter card (*Oo*; page 81)
- picture cards (snow, phone, coat, snowman, toes; pages 100–101)
- blank picture card template (page 83)
- old magazines and workbooks (optional)
- alphabet mini-book (pages 110–111)
- mini-book letter strips (*Oo*; pages 112, 115)

Getting Ready

1. Copy the title and poem onto sentence strips (one line per sentence strip). Highlight the letters that form the long-*o* sound (as indicated above). Place the sentence strips in order in the pocket chart.

2. Photocopy and cut apart the picture cards (snow, phone, coat, snowman, toes). If desired, color them and laminate for durability.

3. Place the picture cards and the letter card (in that order) in the pocket chart across the top.

4. Customize the alphabet mini-book for the letter *Oo*. (See page 5 for directions.)

Teaching With the Pocket Chart Poem

1. Begin by pointing to the picture card for *snow* and asking children to say the name of the picture. Say the word *snow* again, emphasizing the /ō/ sound; have children repeat it. Then write the word *snow* on chart paper (or a whiteboard), and point out that the letters *ow* make the /ō/ sound, which is the long-*o* sound. Continue in the same way with the picture cards for *phone*, *coat*, *snowman*, and *toes*, pointing out that the letters *o_e*, *oa*, and *oe* also make the /ō/ sound.

2. Invite children to get ready to listen to a poem that tells what someone did on a snowy day. As you read the poem and track the print, emphasize the words that have a long-*o* sound. Place the picture cards alongside corresponding lines to reinforce sound-letter associations. When you read the poem a second time, pause after each line or pair of lines. Let children take turns at the chart pointing to and saying each word that has a long-*o* sound. Then read each word aloud with the group. Be sure to point out that in the words *go* and *almost*, the letter *o* makes the long-*o* sound.

3. Ask children to think of other words with the long-*o* sound—for example, *toad*, *goat*, *boat*, *rose*, *yoyo*, and *doe*. Write their suggestions on sentence strips, and trim to size. Point out the letter or letters in each word that form the long-*o* sound (*oa*, *o_e*, *o*, and *oe*). Make picture cards to match children's new words (using the blank picture card template and pictures you draw or cut from old magazines or workbooks). Place the new word and picture cards in the pocket chart. Keep the pocket chart on display, and encourage children to revisit the poem, pictures, and words over the next few days.

4. Write the letters O and *o* slowly on chart paper (or a whiteboard) to model their formation. Have children follow your movements, using their finger to write the letters on their desk or in the air.

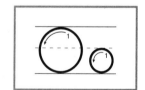

5. Give each child a copy of the alphabet mini-book. Have children use their finger to trace the letter *Oo* in the title. After completing pages 2–4 (see page 5 for directions), invite children to use the back of page 4 (or another sheet of paper) to draw a picture about something that contains the long-*o* sound.

The Letter *Pp*

Pigs and a Pie

A **p**air of little **p**igs

Baked a **p**erfect **p**each **p**ie,

And when it was ready,

They gave it a try.

They cut it in **p**ieces,

And took bite after bite,

And the **p**each **p**ie was gone

By the end of the night!

Materials

- pocket chart
- sentence strips
- letter card (*Pp*; page 81)
- picture cards (pigs, peach, pie; pages 101–102)
- alphabet frame (page 83)
- blank picture card template (page 83)
- old magazines and workbooks (optional)
- alphabet mini-book (pages 110–111)
- mini-book letter strips (*Pp*; pages 112, 115)

Getting Ready

1. Copy the title and poem onto sentence strips (one line per sentence strip). Highlight the letter *Pp* in the initial position (as indicated above). Place the sentence strips in order in the pocket chart.

2. Photocopy and cut apart the picture cards (pigs, peach, pie). If desired, color them and laminate for durability.

3. Place the picture cards and the letter card (in that order) in the pocket chart across the top.

4. Customize the alphabet mini-book for the letter *Pp*. (See page 5 for directions.)

Teaching With the Pocket Chart Poem

1. Begin by pointing to the picture card for *pigs*; ask children what they see. Say the word *pigs*, emphasizing the /p/ sound, and have children repeat it. Then ask what letter of the alphabet makes the /p/ sound. Point to the uppercase and lowercase *Pp* and have children name each letter. Ask them to identify the names of the other pictures that begin with the /p/ sound and the letter *p* (peach, pie).

2. Invite children to get ready to listen to a poem about two little pigs that bake a pie. As you read the poem, emphasize those words that begin with the /p/ sound. Place the picture cards alongside corresponding lines to reinforce sound-letter associations. When you read the poem a second time, pause after each pair of lines. Invite volunteers to take turns using the alphabet frame to isolate each letter *p* that begins a word and represents the /p/ sound. Together, read these words aloud.

3. Ask children to think of other words that begin with the /p/ sound and the letter *p*—for example, *puppy, puzzle, pen, paint,* and *paper*. Write their suggestions on sentence strips, and trim to size. Make picture cards to match children's new words (using the blank picture card template and pictures you draw or cut from old magazines or workbooks). Place the new word and picture cards in the pocket chart. Keep the pocket chart on display, and encourage children to revisit the poem, pictures, and words over the next few days.

4. Write the letters *P* and *p* slowly on chart paper (or a whiteboard) to model their formation. Have children follow your movements by using their finger to write each letter on their palm.

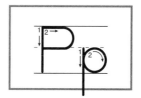

5. Give each child a copy of the alphabet mini-book. Have children use their finger to trace the letter *Pp* in the title. After completing pages 2–4 (see page 5 for directions), invite children to use the back of page 4 (or another sheet of paper) to draw a picture of the two little pigs enjoying something else that begins with the /p/ sound, such as pancakes, popcorn, or pickles.

The Letter Qq

A Quilt for the Queen

One day when the weather outside was cold,

And the **q**ueen began to shiver,

She wrapped herself in a **q**uilt of gold,

And no longer did she **q**uiver.

The golden **q**uilt kept the **q**ueen **q**uite warm,

In fact, as warm as toast.

It **q**uickly became her favorite thing,

She loved her **q**uilt the most!

Materials

❁ pocket chart

❁ sentence strips

❁ letter card (*Qq*; page 81)

❁ picture cards (queen, quilt; page 102)

❁ alphabet frame (page 83)

❁ blank picture card template (page 83)

❁ old magazines and workbooks (optional)

❁ alphabet mini-book (pages 110–111)

❁ mini-book letter strips (*Qq*; pages 112, 116)

Getting Ready

1. Copy the title and poem onto sentence strips (one line per sentence strip). Highlight the letter *Qq* in the initial position (as indicated above). Place the sentence strips in order in the pocket chart.

2. Photocopy and cut apart the picture cards (queen, quilt). If desired, color them and laminate for durability.

3. Place the picture cards and the letter card (in that order) in the pocket chart across the top.

4. Customize the alphabet mini-book for the letter *Qq*. (See page 5 for directions.)

Teaching With the Pocket Chart Poem

1. Begin by pointing to the picture card for *queen*, and ask children what they see. Say the word *queen*, emphasizing the /kw/ sound, and have children repeat it. Then ask what letters of the alphabet make the /kw/ sound. Explain that in English, the letter *q* in a word is always followed by the letter *u*. Point to the uppercase and lowercase *Qq* and have children name each letter. Ask children to identify the other picture whose name begins with the /kw/ sound and the letter *q* (quilt).

2. Tell children that they will be listening to a poem about a queen and her quilt. As you read the poem, stress the words that begin with the /kw/ sound. Place the picture cards alongside corresponding lines to reinforce sound-letter associations. When you read the poem a second time, pause after each pair of lines. Invite volunteers to take turns using the alphabet frame to isolate the letters *qu* that represent the /kw/ sound. Together, read these words aloud.

3. Ask children to think of other words that begin with the /kw/ sound and the letters *qu*—for example, *quiet*, *quiz*, *quack*, *quarter*, and *question*. Write their suggestions on sentence strips, and trim to size. Make picture cards to match children's new words (using the blank picture card template and pictures you draw or cut from old magazines or workbooks). Place the new word and picture cards in the pocket chart. Keep the pocket chart on display, and encourage children to revisit the poem, pictures, and words over the next few days.

4. Write the letters *Q* and *q* slowly on chart paper (or a whiteboard) to model their formation. Have children follow your movements by writing the letters in the air.

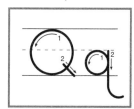

5. Give each child a copy of the alphabet mini-book. Have children use their finger to trace the letter *Qq* in the title. After completing pages 2–4 (see page 5 for directions), invite children to use the back of page 4 (or another sheet of paper) to draw a picture of the queen fast asleep in her bed, covered with her golden quilt.

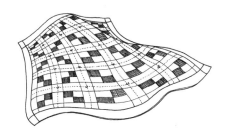

The Letter *Rr*

A Rhyme About Red

Roses are **r**ed,
Raspberries too,
So is a **r**adish,
That names a few.
There's **r**ed in a **r**ainbow,
And in a **r**ooster's comb.
Now you've come to the end
Of this **r**hyming **r**ed poem!

Materials

🌸 pocket chart

🌸 sentence strips

🌸 letter card (*Rr*; page 81)

🌸 picture cards (roses, raspberries, radish, rainbow, rooster; pages 102–103)

🌸 alphabet frame (page 83)

🌸 blank picture card template (page 83)

🌸 old magazines and workbooks (optional)

🌸 alphabet mini-book (pages 110–111)

🌸 mini-book letter strips (*Rr*; pages 112, 116)

Getting Ready

1. Copy the title and poem onto sentence strips (one line per sentence strip). Highlight the letter *Rr* in the initial position (as indicated above). Place the sentence strips in order in the pocket chart.

2. Photocopy and cut apart the picture cards (roses, raspberries, radish, rainbow, rooster). If desired, color them and laminate for durability.

3. Place the picture cards and the letter card (in that order) in the pocket chart across the top.

4. Customize the alphabet mini-book for the letter *Rr*. (See page 5 for directions.)

Teaching With the Pocket Chart Poem

1. Point to the picture card for *roses*, and ask children what they see. Say the word *roses*, emphasizing the /r/ sound; have children repeat it. Then ask: *What letter of the alphabet makes the /r/ sound?* Point to the uppercase and lowercase *Rr* and have children name each letter. Invite them to identify the names of the other pictures that begin with the /r/ sound and the letter *r* (raspberries, radish, rainbow, rooster).

2. Invite children to get ready to listen to a poem about things that are red. As you read the poem, emphasize the words that begin with the /r/ sound. Place the picture cards alongside corresponding lines to reinforce sound-letter associations. When you read the poem a second time, pause after each pair of lines. Invite volunteers to take turns using the alphabet frame to isolate each letter *r* that begins a word and represents the /r/ sound. Together, read these words aloud.

3. Ask children to think of other words that begin with the /r/ sound and the letter *r*—for example, *rabbit, run, read, rug,* and *ring*. Write their suggestions on sentence strips, and trim to size. Make picture cards to match children's new words (using the blank picture card template and pictures you draw or cut from old magazines or workbooks). Place the new word and picture cards in the pocket chart. Keep the pocket chart on display, and encourage children to revisit the poem, pictures, and words over the next few days.

4. Write the letters *R* and *r* slowly on chart paper (or a whiteboard) to model their formation. Have children follow your movements by taking turns and using their finger to write each letter on a partner's back.

5. Give each child a copy of the alphabet mini-book. Have children use their finger to trace the letter *Rr* in the title. After completing pages 2–4 (see page 5 for directions), invite children to use the back of page 4 (or another sheet of paper) to draw a picture of themselves wearing a red raincoat, and walking in the rain. Children might like to add other details to their pictures that represent the letter *Rr*, such as a road, a rabbit, and a rose garden.

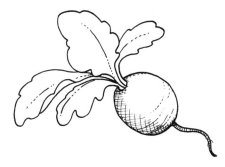

The Letter Ss

Sammy Seal

Sammy **S**eal likes to **s**ing
This very happy **s**ong:
"I like the **s**un,
I like the **s**ea,
I'm **s**ailing all day long!"

Materials

- pocket chart
- sentence strips
- letter card (*Ss*; page 82)
- picture cards (seal, sun, sea; page 104)
- alphabet frame (page 83)
- blank picture card template (page 83)
- old magazines and workbooks (optional)
- alphabet mini-book (pages 110–111)
- mini-book letter strips (*Ss*; pages 112, 116)

Getting Ready

1. Copy the title and poem onto sentence strips (one line per sentence strip). Highlight the letter *Ss* in the initial position (as indicated above). Place the sentence strips in order in the pocket chart.

2. Photocopy and cut apart the picture cards (seal, sun, sea). If desired, color them and laminate for durability.

3. Place the picture cards and the letter card (in that order) in the pocket chart across the top.

4. Customize the alphabet mini-book for the letter *Ss*. (See page 5 for directions.)

Teaching With the Pocket Chart Poem

1. Point to the picture card for *seal*, and ask children what they see. Say the word *seal*, emphasizing the /s/ sound; have children repeat it. Then ask: *What letter of the alphabet makes the /s/ sound?* Point to the uppercase and lowercase *Ss* and have children name each letter. Ask them to identify the names of the other pictures that begin with the /s/ sound and the letter *s* (sun, sea).

2. Invite children to get ready to listen to a poem about a seal named Sammy. As you read the poem, emphasize the words that begin with the /s/ sound. Place the picture cards alongside corresponding lines to reinforce sound-letter associations. When you read the poem a second time, pause after each pair of lines. Invite volunteers to take turns using the alphabet frame to isolate each letter *s* that begins a word and represents the /s/ sound. Together, read these words aloud.

3. Ask children to think of other words that begin with the /s/ sound and the letter *s*—for example, *sailboat, sand, sock, sandal,* and *six*. Write their suggestions on sentence strips, and trim to size. Make picture cards to match children's new words (using the blank picture card template and pictures you draw or cut from old magazines or workbooks). Place the new word and picture cards in the pocket chart. Keep the pocket chart on display, and encourage children to revisit the poem, pictures, and words over the next few days.

4. Write the letters S and s slowly on chart paper (or a whiteboard) to model their formation. Have children follow your movements, using their finger to write the letters in the air or on their palms.

5. Give each child a copy of the alphabet mini-book. Have children use their finger to trace the letter *Ss* in the title. After completing pages 2–4 (see page 5 for directions), invite children to use the back of page 4 (or another sheet of paper) to draw a picture of Sammy Seal eating a sandwich on his sailboat.

The Letter *Tt*

My Toy Tiger

I have a **t**oy **t**iger
That I **t**ake **t**o bed each night,
And if we see a shadow move,
We hug each other **t**ight.
We cuddle up **t**ogether
As we look out at the moon,
And **t**ill it's **t**ime **t**o fall asleep,
We sing a happy **t**une!

Materials

- pocket chart
- sentence strips
- letter card (*Tt*; page 82)
- picture card (tiger; page 104)
- alphabet frame (page 83)
- blank picture card template (page 83)
- old magazines and workbooks (optional)
- alphabet mini-book (pages 110–111)
- mini-book letter strips (*Tt*; pages 112, 116)

Getting Ready

1. Copy the title and poem onto sentence strips (one line per sentence strip). Highlight the letter *Tt* in the initial position (as indicated above). Place the sentence strips in order in the pocket chart.

2. Photocopy and cut apart the picture card (tiger). If desired, color it and laminate for durability.

3. Place the picture card and the letter card (in that order) in the pocket chart across the top.

4. Customize the alphabet mini-book for the letter *Tt*. (See page 5 for directions.)

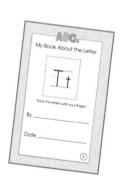

Teaching With the Pocket Chart Poem

1. Begin by pointing to the picture card for *tiger*, and ask children what they see. Say the word *tiger*, emphasizing the /t/ sound; have children repeat it. Then ask: *What letter of the alphabet makes the /t/ sound?* Point to the uppercase and lowercase *Tt* and have children name each letter. Ask them to point to and name something else in the picture that begins with the /t/ sound and the letter *t* (tail).

2. Invite children to get ready to listen to a poem about a toy tiger. As you read the poem, emphasize those words that begin with the /t/ sound. Place the picture card alongside the corresponding line to reinforce sound-letter associations. When you read the poem a second time, pause after each pair of lines. Invite volunteers to take turns using the alphabet frame to isolate each letter *t* that begins a word and represents the /t/ sound. Together, read these words aloud.

3. Ask children to think of other words that begin with the /t/ sound and the letter *t*—for example, *teeth, toothbrush, turtle,* and *toys*. Write their suggestions on sentence strips, and trim to size. Make picture cards to match children's new words (using the blank picture card template and pictures you draw or cut from old magazines or workbooks). Place the new word and picture cards in the pocket chart. Keep the pocket chart on display, and encourage children to revisit the poem, pictures, and words over the next few days.

4. Write the letters *T* and *t* slowly on chart paper (or a whiteboard) to model their formation. Have children follow your movements by using their finger to write each letter on their palm.

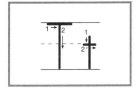

5. Give each child a copy of the alphabet mini-book. Have children use their finger to trace the letter *Tt* in the title. After completing pages 2–4 (see page 5 for directions), invite children to use the back of page 4 (or another sheet of paper) to draw a picture of the tiger and a teddy bear doing something that begins with *t*, such as talking on the telephone or having toast and tea.

The Letter **Uu** (short *u*)

Under an Umbrella

When the rain comes down,
D**u**ck's **u**mbrella goes **u**p,
And **u**nder the **u**mbrella
Hurry C**u**b and little P**u**p.
They hold each other tight,
And together they h**u**ddle,
And they have a lot of f**u**n
As they j**u**mp across each p**u**ddle!

Materials

🎴 pocket chart

🎴 sentence strips

🎴 letter card (*Uu*; page 82)

🎴 picture cards (duck, umbrella, bear cub, puppy, puddle; pages 105–106)

🎴 alphabet frame (page 83)

🎴 blank picture card template (page 83)

🎴 old magazines and workbooks (optional)

🎴 alphabet mini-book (pages 110–111)

🎴 mini-book letter strips (*Uu*; pages 112, 116)

Getting Ready

1. Copy the title and poem onto sentence strips (one line per sentence strip). Highlight the letter *Uu* in the initial and medial position (as indicated above). Place the sentence strips in order in the pocket chart.

2. Photocopy and cut apart the picture cards (duck, umbrella, bear cub, puppy, puddle). If desired, color them and laminate for durability.

3. Place the picture cards and the letter card (in that order) in the pocket chart across the top.

4. Customize the alphabet mini-book for the letter *Uu*. (See page 5 for directions.)

Teaching With the Pocket Chart Poem

1. Begin by pointing to the picture card for *umbrella*, and ask children what they see. Say the word *umbrella*, stressing the /u/ sound, and have children repeat it. Then ask: *What letter of the alphabet makes the /u/ sound?* Point to the uppercase and lowercase *Uu* and have children name each letter.

2. Explain: *Sometimes the /u/ sound comes in the middle of a word.* Point to the picture card for *duck* and have children say the word. Ask: *What sound do you hear in the middle of duck?* (/u/) *What letter makes the /u/ sound?* (*u*) Ask children to identify the other pictures whose names have the /u/ sound in the middle (puppy or pup, puddle).

3. Invite children to get ready to listen to a poem about a duck, her umbrella, and her two friends. As you read the poem, emphasize words that have an initial or a medial /u/ sound. Place the picture cards alongside corresponding lines to reinforce sound-letter associations. When you read the poem a second time, pause after each pair of lines. Invite volunteers to take turns using the alphabet frame to isolate each letter *u* that represents the /u/ sound. Together, read these words aloud.

4. Ask children to think of other words that are like *umbrella* and begin with the /u/ sound and the letter *u*, such as *uncle*, *us*, and *until*. Repeat for words that are like *cub* and have the /u/ sound and the letter *u* in the middle, such as *truck*, *drum*, and *hug*. Write their suggestions on sentence strips, and trim to size. Make picture cards to match children's new words (using the blank picture card template and pictures you draw or cut from old magazines or workbooks). Place the new word and picture cards in the pocket chart. Keep the pocket chart on display, and encourage children to revisit the poem, pictures, and words over the next few days.

5. Write the letters *U* and *u* slowly on chart paper (or a whiteboard) to model their formation. Have children follow your movements by writing each letter in the air.

6. Give each child a copy of the alphabet mini-book. Have children use their finger to trace the letter *Uu* in the title. After completing pages 2–4 (see page 5 for directions), invite children to use the back of page 4 (or another sheet of paper) to draw a picture of themselves under an umbrella with Duck, Cub, and Pup, jumping across a puddle.

The Letter **Uu** (long *u*)

A Mule Named Sue

Listen to a story that's tr**ue**

About a m**u**l**e** whose name is S**ue**.

She sings and plays the fl**u**t**e**.

She wears a funny s**ui**t!

Her sister's name is R**u**th.

She plays the t**u**ba—that's the tr**u**th!

These sisters are quite a c**u**t**e** pair.

They play m**u**sic everywhere!

Materials

 pocket chart

 sentence strips

 letter card (*Uu*; page 82)

 picture cards (mule, flute, suit, tuba, music; pages 106–107)

 blank picture card template (page 83)

 old magazines and workbooks (optional)

 alphabet mini-book (pages 110–111)

 mini-book letter strips (*Uu*; pages 112, 116)

Getting Ready

1. Copy the title and poem onto sentence strips (one line per sentence strip). Highlight the letters that form the long-*u* sound (as indicated above). Place the sentence strips in order in the pocket chart.

2. Photocopy and cut apart the picture cards (mule, flute, suit, tuba, music). If desired, color them and laminate for durability.

3. Place the picture cards and the letter card (in that order) in the pocket chart across the top.

4. Customize the alphabet mini-book for the letter *Uu*. (See page 5 for directions.)

Teaching With the Pocket Chart Poem

A Note About the Long-*u* Sound: In this lesson, as in many phonics programs, we teach that the vowel sounds in *flute* and *mule* both represent the long-*u* sound. Explain to children that the /o͞o/ sound in the words *true, Sue, flute, suit, Ruth, tuba, truth* and the /yo͞o/ or /ū/ sound in the words *mule, cute,* and *music* are both considered long-*u* sounds.

1. Begin by pointing to the picture card for *mule* and asking children to say the name of the picture. Say the word *mule* again, emphasizing the /yo͞o/ sound; have children repeat it. Then write the word *mule* on chart paper (or a whiteboard), and point out that the letters *u_e* make the /yo͞o/ sound, which is the long-*u* sound. Point to the picture card for *music*, and write the word on chart paper. Point out that the letter *u* in *music* makes the /yo͞o/ sound as well. Continue in the same way with the picture cards for *flute, suit,* and *tuba*, pointing out that the /o͞o/ sound in these words is also called the long-*u* sound.

2. Invite children to get ready to listen to a poem about a mule named Sue and her sister, Ruth. As you read the poem and track the print, emphasize words with the long-*u* sound. Place the picture cards alongside corresponding lines to reinforce sound-letter associations. When you reread the poem, pause after each line or pair of lines. Let children take turns at the chart pointing to and saying each word that has a long-*u* sound. Then read each word aloud with the group. Point out that in the words *Sue* and *true*, the letters *ue* make the long-*u* sound.

3. Ask children to think of other words with the long-*u* sound—for example, *cube, ruler, fruit,* and *blue*. Write their suggestions on sentence strips, and trim to size. Point out the letters in each word that form the long-*u* sound (*u_e, ui,* and *ue*). Make picture cards to match children's new words (using the blank picture card template and pictures you draw or cut from old magazines or workbooks). Place the new word and picture cards in the pocket chart. Keep the pocket chart on display so that children can revisit it over the next few days.

4. Write the letters *U* and *u* slowly on chart paper (or a whiteboard) to model their formation. Have children follow your movements by writing each letter in the air.

5. Give each child a copy of the alphabet mini-book. Have children use their finger to trace the letter *Uu* in the title. After completing pages 2–4 (see page 5 for directions), invite children to use the back of page 4 (or another sheet of paper) to draw something else that Sue and Ruth might do, such as measure with a ruler (matching picture choices with the long-*u* sound).

The Letter Vv

Victor and His Violin

Victor played the **v**iolin.

He was the **v**ery best.

And when he went onstage to play,

He wore his lucky **v**est.

One day his **v**est did **v**anish,

And **V**ictor understood

That even without his lucky **v**est,

His playing was just as good!

Materials

❧ pocket chart

❧ sentence strips

❧ letter card (*Vv*; page 82)

❧ picture cards (violin, vest; page 107)

❧ alphabet frame (page 83)

❧ blank picture card template (page 83)

❧ old magazines and workbooks (optional)

❧ alphabet mini-book (pages 110–111)

❧ mini-book letter strips (*Vv*; pages 112, 117)

Getting Ready

1. Copy the title and poem onto sentence strips (one line per sentence strip). Highlight the letter *Vv* in the initial position (as indicated above). Place the sentence strips in order in the pocket chart.

2. Photocopy and cut apart the picture cards (violin, vest). If desired, color them and laminate for durability.

3. Place the picture cards and the letter card (in that order) in the pocket chart across the top.

4. Customize the alphabet mini-book for the letter *Vv*. (See page 5 for directions.)

Teaching With the Pocket Chart Poem

1. Point to the picture card for *violin*, and ask children what they see. Say the word *violin*, stressing the /v/ sound; have children repeat it. Ask: *What letter of the alphabet makes the /v/ sound?* Point to the uppercase and lowercase Vv and have children name each letter. Then have them name the other picture that begins with the /v/ sound and the letter *v* (vest).

2. Invite children to get ready to listen to a poem about a boy named Victor who played the violin. As you read the poem, emphasize the words that begin with the /v/ sound. Place the picture cards alongside corresponding lines to reinforce sound-letter associations. When you read the poem a second time, pause after each pair of lines. Invite volunteers to take turns using the alphabet frame to isolate each letter *v* that begins a word and represents the /v/ sound. Together, read these words aloud.

3. Ask children to think of other words that begin with the /v/ sound and the letter *v*—for example, *vet*, *van*, *vegetables*, and *volcano*. Write their suggestions on sentence strips, and trim to size. Make picture cards to match children's new words (using the blank picture card template and pictures you draw or cut from old magazines or workbooks). Place the new word and picture cards in the pocket chart. Keep the pocket chart on display, and encourage children to revisit the poem, pictures, and words over the next few days.

4. Write the letters V and v slowly on chart paper (or a whiteboard) to model their formation. Have children follow your movements by taking turns and using their finger to write each letter on a partner's back.

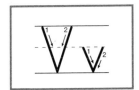

5. Give each child a copy of the alphabet mini-book. Have children use their finger to trace the letter Vv in the title. After completing pages 2–4 (see page 5 for directions), invite children to use the back of page 4 (or another sheet of paper) to draw a picture about something that contains the letter Vv. For example, they might draw themselves wearing a vest and eating a vanilla ice cream cone. They can add details such as a vase with flowers, a bowl of vegetables, and a "painting" of a volcano on the wall.

The Letter Ww

Silly Willy Walrus

Willy the **w**alrus is silly,

His friends **w**ill often say,

Because he always **w**ants to **w**ear

A different **w**ig each day.

"I'm not so **w**acky!" **W**illy says,

"I don't mind if you stare.

I **w**ould rather **w**ear a **w**ig each day,

Than leave my poor head bare!"

Materials

❧ pocket chart

❧ sentence strips

❧ letter card (*Ww*; page 82)

❧ picture cards (walrus, wig; page 108)

❧ alphabet frame (page 83)

❧ blank picture card template (page 83)

❧ old magazines and workbooks (optional)

❧ alphabet mini-book (pages 110–111)

❧ mini-book letter strips (*Ww*; pages 112, 117)

Getting Ready

1. Copy the title and poem onto sentence strips (one line per sentence strip). Highlight the letter *Ww* in the initial position (as indicated above). Place the sentence strips in order in the pocket chart.

2. Photocopy and cut apart the picture cards (walrus, wig). If desired, color them and laminate for durability.

3. Place the picture cards and the letter card (in that order) in the pocket chart across the top.

4. Customize the alphabet mini-book for the letter *Ww*. (See page 5 for directions.)

Teaching With the Pocket Chart Poem

1. Point to the picture card for *walrus*, and ask children what they see. Say the word *walrus*, emphasizing the /w/ sound; have children repeat it. Ask: *What letter of the alphabet makes the /w/ sound?* Point to the uppercase and lowercase *Ww* and have children name each letter. Then ask them to name the other picture whose name begins with the /w/ sound and the letter *w* (wig).

2. Tell children to get ready to listen to a poem about a walrus named Willy. As you read the poem, emphasize words that begin with the /w/ sound. Place the picture cards alongside corresponding lines to reinforce sound-letter associations. When you read the poem a second time, pause after each pair of lines. Invite volunteers to take turns using the alphabet frame to isolate each letter *w* that begins a word and represents the /w/ sound. Together, read these words aloud.

3. Ask children to think of other words that begin with the /w/ sound and the letter *w*—for example, *wagon, window, wall, word,* and *wet*. Write their suggestions on sentence strips, and trim to size. Make picture cards to match children's new words (using the blank picture card template and pictures you draw or cut from old magazines or workbooks). Place the new word and picture cards in the pocket chart. Keep the pocket chart on display, and encourage children to revisit the poem, pictures, and words over the next few days.

4. Write the letters *W* and *w* slowly on chart paper (or a whiteboard) to model their formation. Have children follow your movements, writing each letter in the air.

5. Give each child a copy of the alphabet mini-book. Have children use their finger to trace the letter *Ww* in the title. After completing pages 2–4 (see page 5 for directions), invite children to use the back of page 4 (or another sheet of paper) to draw a picture of Willy the walrus wearing a funny wig.

The Letter Xx

Fix It Fox!

There once was a fo**x** named Andy,

With his toolbo**x**, he was handy.

In si**x** minutes flat,

He could fi**x** this and that,

And then everything would be dandy!

Materials

- pocket chart
- sentence strips
- letter card (*Xx*; page 82)
- picture cards (fox, toolbox, 6; pages 108–109)
- alphabet frame (page 83)
- blank picture card template (page 83)
- old magazines and workbooks (optional)
- alphabet mini-book (pages 110–111)
- mini-book letter strips (*Xx*; pages 112, 117)

Getting Ready

1. Copy the title and poem onto sentence strips (one line per sentence strip). Highlight the letter *Xx* in the final position (as indicated above). Place the sentence strips in order in the pocket chart.

2. Photocopy and cut apart the picture cards (fox, toolbox, 6). If desired, color them and laminate for durability.

3. Place the picture cards and the letter card (in that order) in the pocket chart across the top.

4. Customize the alphabet mini-book for the letter *Xx*. (See page 5 for directions.)

Teaching With the Pocket Chart Poem

1. Begin by pointing to the picture card for *fox*, and ask children what they see. Then say: *Today you will be listening for the sound at the end of a word.* Say the word *fox*, emphasizing the /ks/ sound, and have children repeat it. Then ask: *What letter of the alphabet makes the /ks/ sound?* Point to the uppercase and lowercase *Xx* and have children name each letter. Ask them to identify the other pictures whose names end with the /ks/ sound and the letter *x* (toolbox, six).

2. Tell children they are going to listen to a poem about a fox named Andy who could fix anything. As you read the poem, emphasize those words that end with the /ks/ sound. Place the picture cards alongside corresponding lines to reinforce sound-letter associations. When you read the poem a second time, pause after each pair of lines. Invite volunteers to take turns using the alphabet frame to isolate each letter *x* that represents the /ks/ sound. Together, read these words aloud.

3. Ask children to think of other words that end with the /ks/ sound and the letter *x*—for example, *ax, mix, relax, ox,* and *wax*. Write their suggestions on sentence strips, and trim to size. Make picture cards to match children's new words (using the blank picture card template and pictures you draw or cut from old magazines or workbooks). Place the new word and picture cards in the pocket chart. Keep the pocket chart on display, and encourage children to revisit the poem, pictures, and words over the next few days.

4. Write the letters X and x slowly on chart paper (or a whiteboard) to model their formation. Have children follow your movements by using their finger to write each letter on their palm.

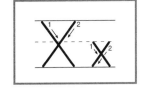

5. Give each child a copy of the alphabet mini-book. Have children use their finger to trace the letter *Xx* in the title. After completing pages 2–4 (see page 5 for directions), invite children to use the back of page 4 (or another sheet of paper) to draw a picture of Andy the fox with his toolbox, painting a mailbox.

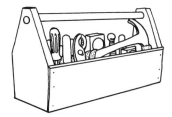

The Letter Yy

A Snack for a Yak

Yesterday I looked out,
And what did I see?
A **y**ak in my **y**ard!
But how could that be?
I **y**elled to my mom,
"Do **y**ou see that big **y**ak?"
"**Y**es, dear," she said.
"He just wants a snack!"

Materials

🌸 pocket chart

🌸 sentence strips

🌸 letter card (*Yy*; page 83)

🌸 picture cards (yak, yard; page 109)

🌸 alphabet frame (page 83)

🌸 blank picture card template (page 83)

🌸 old magazines and workbooks (optional)

🌸 alphabet mini-book (pages 110–111)

🌸 mini-book letter strips (*Yy*; pages 112, 117)

Getting Ready

1. Copy the title and poem onto sentence strips (one line per sentence strip). Highlight the letter Yy in the initial position (as indicated above). Place the sentence strips in order in the pocket chart.

2. Photocopy and cut apart the picture cards (yak, yard). If desired, color them and laminate for durability.

3. Place the picture cards and the letter card (in that order) in the pocket chart across the top.

4. Customize the alphabet mini-book for the letter Yy. (See page 5 for directions.)

Teaching With the Pocket Chart Poem

1. Point to the picture card for *yak*, and ask children what they see. Explain that a yak is a large, long-haired ox. Say the word *yak*, emphasizing the /y/ sound; have children repeat it. Then ask: *What letter of the alphabet makes the /y/ sound?* Point to the uppercase and lowercase Yy and have children name each letter. Ask children to identify the other picture whose name begins with the /y/ sound and the letter y (yard).

2. Invite children to get ready to listen to a poem about a child who sees a yak in the yard. As you read the poem, emphasize words that begin with the /y/ sound. Place the picture cards alongside corresponding lines to reinforce sound-letter associations. When you read the poem a second time, pause after each pair of lines. Invite volunteers to take turns using the alphabet frame to isolate each letter y that begins the word and represents the /y/ sound. Together, read these words aloud.

3. Ask children to think of other words that begin with the /y/ sound and the letter y—for example, *yellow, year, yarn, yolk,* and *yawn.* Write their suggestions on sentence strips, and trim to size. Make picture cards to match children's new words (using the blank picture card template and pictures you draw or cut from old magazines or workbooks). Place the new word and picture cards in the pocket chart. Keep the pocket chart on display, and encourage children to revisit the poem, pictures, and words over the next few days.

4. Write the letters Y and y slowly on chart paper (or a whiteboard) to model their formation. Have children follow your movements by writing each letter in the air.

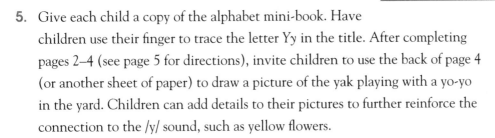

5. Give each child a copy of the alphabet mini-book. Have children use their finger to trace the letter Yy in the title. After completing pages 2–4 (see page 5 for directions), invite children to use the back of page 4 (or another sheet of paper) to draw a picture of the yak playing with a yo-yo in the yard. Children can add details to their pictures to further reinforce the connection to the /y/ sound, such as yellow flowers.

The Letter Zz

Zoom to the Zoo!

Whenever I go to the **z**oo,

The thing that I like to do

Is **z**oom to the **z**ebras' park,

And watch **z**ebras until it gets dark.

Monkeys are funny and **z**any,

And lions can certainly roar,

But for me the best sight

In their suits black and white

Are the **z**ebras—of that I am sure!

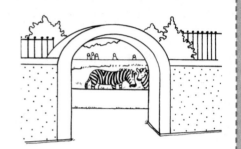

Materials

- pocket chart
- sentence strips
- letter card (*Zz*; page 83)
- picture card (zoo/zebras; page 109)
- alphabet frame (page 83)
- blank picture card template (page 83)
- old magazines and workbooks (optional)
- alphabet mini-book (pages 110–111)
- mini-book letter strips (*Zz*; pages 112, 117)

Getting Ready

1. Copy the title and poem onto sentence strips (one line per sentence strip). Highlight the letter *Zz* in the initial position (as indicated above). Place the sentence strips in order in the pocket chart.

2. Photocopy and cut apart the picture card (zoo/zebras). If desired, color it and laminate for durability.

3. Place the picture cards and the letter card (in that order) in the pocket chart across the top.

4. Customize the alphabet mini-book for the letter *Zz*. (See page 5 for directions.)

Teaching With the Pocket Chart Poem

1. Point to the picture; ask children to name the place pictured. Say the word *zoo*, emphasizing the /z/ sound; have children repeat it. Then ask: *What letter of the alphabet makes the /z/ sound?* Point to the uppercase and lowercase Zz and have children name each letter. Ask them to name what they see at the zoo that begins with the /z/ sound and the letter z (zebras).

2. Invite children to get ready to listen to a poem about someone who likes to visit the zebras at the zoo. As you read the poem, emphasize words that begin with the /z/ sound. Place the picture card alongside a corresponding line to reinforce sound-letter associations. When you read the poem a second time, pause after each pair of lines. Invite volunteers to take turns using the alphabet frame to isolate each letter z that begins a word and represents the /z/ sound. Together, read these words aloud.

3. Ask children to think of other words that begin with the /z/ sound and the letter z—for example, *zipper, zero, zigzag,* and *zucchini.* Write their suggestions on sentence strips, and trim to size. Make picture cards to match children's new words (using the blank picture card template and pictures you draw or cut from old magazines or workbooks). Place the new word and picture cards in the pocket chart. Keep the pocket chart on display, and encourage children to revisit the poem, pictures, and words over the next few days.

4. Write the letters Z and z slowly on chart paper (or a whiteboard) to model their formation. Have children follow your movements by taking turns using their finger to write each letter on a partner's back.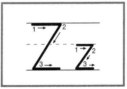

5. Give each child a copy of the alphabet mini-book. Have children use their finger to trace the letter Zz in the title. After completing pages 2–4 (see page 5 for directions), invite children to use the back of page 4 (or another sheet of paper) to draw a picture of themselves visiting zebras at the zoo.

Activities and Games
for Every Letter

Open-Ended ABC Pocket Chart Poem

To practice a specific letter-sound relationship, write the following poem on sentence strips, placing any letter of the alphabet in the blank spaces:

Let's learn the letter __ today.

We'll put it in our chart.

Let's say some words that start with __,

And we can all look smart!

Ask children to name some words that begin with that specific sound and letter. Write the words on sentence strips, trim to size, and have children make picture cards to go with them. You can mix up the cards and have children match them to reinforce word recognition.

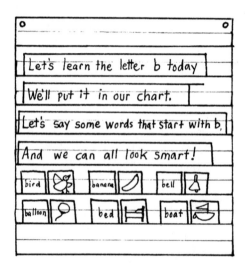

Sounds and Letters

Place five pictures in the pocket chart. Use the picture cards (pages 84–109 and 160–170) or pictures from magazines, old workbooks, or clip art that you have on hand. Each picture name should begin with a different sound/letter. Below the pictures, in mixed-up order, place the five initial letters. Then say, for example: *Find the picture whose name begins with the /l/ sound. Now find the letter that makes that sound.* Repeat to match all pictures and letters. Then continue with a new set of pictures and letters.

Open-Ended Pocket Chart Poem for Names

Write the following poem on sentence strips and place it in the pocket chart:

My name begins with the letter ___,

I'm very proud to say.

And I can tell you three more words

That begin the very same way!

Give each child the opportunity to recite the poem and insert the appropriate uppercase letter in the first line. Write the three words that each child names on sentence strips, and trim to size. You may want to expand the activity by creating a bulletin board of names and words. Have children write their name on a sheet of drawing paper, making the first letter decorative and special. Place children's word cards beneath their name.

Open-Ended Pocket Chart Riddle

Write the following rhyming riddle on sentence strips and place it in the pocket chart:

I'm thinking of a letter.

Do you think you know the one?

It begins the word _____.

And now this riddle is done!

Ask a child to think of a letter and a word that begins with that letter. Have the child recite the riddle to the group. The other children must name the letter that the word begins with. As an alternative, you may want to change the third line of the riddle to read: "It makes the sound _____."

ABC Match

Place the uppercase letters of the alphabet in the top section of the pocket chart and the lowercase letters below them. (Place the letters in order or mix them up for a challenge.) Randomly call out the name of a letter and invite a volunteer to find the uppercase and lowercase letters. Have the child hold them up for the class and name them. Continue until all the letter partners have been taken from the pocket chart.

Point to the Letter

Fill the pocket chart with the uppercase and lowercase letters of the alphabet. Use as many sets of letters as you need to fill the entire chart. Place the pocket chart so that it is accessible to children. Invite volunteers to come to the chart, cover their eyes, and put their finger on the chart. When they open their eyes, they tell what letter they are pointing to and what sound the letter makes. If they like, children can also say a word that begins with that sound and letter.

Sing the Alphabet Song

Place the uppercase letters of the alphabet in the pocket chart. Begin by having children sing the alphabet song once or twice, as you point to the letters in the chart. Then say: *We're going to sing the alphabet song again, but this time stand up when we say the letter at the beginning of your name.* After all children are standing, repeat the song and have children sit down when the letter that begins their name is sung.

What's in the Picture?

Review letter-sound relationships by selecting a pocket chart picture for any alphabet letter. Have children name the object in the picture (such as *daisy*), say the initial sound (/d/), and place the initial letter card (*Dd*) in the pocket chart below the picture. Children may then find other picture cards that go with this letter and add them to the pocket chart.

Picture Sort

Select two letters that do not have similar sounds, such as *b* and *r* or *w* and *k*. Place a letter at the top of each side (left, right) of the pocket chart. Select four or five pictures that begin with the sound of each letter and mix them together. Use picture cards in this book (pages 84–109 and 160–170) or pictures from magazines, old workbooks, or clip art that you have on hand. Have children choose a picture, say the word, and place the picture under the corresponding letter.

Find the Missing Letters

Place the lowercase letters of the alphabet in the pocket chart with several letters missing—for example, *a, b, d, e, f, g, i, j, k, m, n, p, q, r, t, u, w, y, z*. Have children identify the missing letters (*c, h, l, o, s, v, x*) and place each letter in the appropriate place. Play several rounds, choosing new missing letters each time. Repeat, using the uppercase letters of the alphabet.

Name Bingo

Ask each child to write his or her name on a sheet of paper. Then randomly place alphabet letters in the pocket chart, one at a time, and have children identify them. Explain to children that when a letter is shown that appears in their name, they should cross out that letter. When all the letters are crossed out in someone's name, he or she is the winner of Name Bingo!

Exercises for Uppercase and Lowercase Letters

Place an uppercase or a lowercase letter in the pocket chart. Explain that when children see an uppercase letter, they must stand on tiptoes, stretch their arms up in the air, and say the letter name. When they see a lowercase letter, they must squat, hug their knees, and say the letter name.

Musical Letter Match

Have children form two circles, one inside the other. Give each child in the inner circle an uppercase letter card. Give each child in the outer circle a corresponding lowercase letter card. Play some lively music and have children march in their circles. As soon as the music stops, children should find their partner letters and hold the cards up high!

Building Words

Select a picture that represents a CVC word—for example, a picture of a cat. Use pictures from magazines or clip art that you have on hand. Beneath the picture, place the letters *at* and say the sounds: /a/-/t/. Ask children to identify the initial sound and letter that will complete the word *cat*. Place this letter in the correct position in the pocket chart and read the word together. Continue with other pictures whose names end with the same phonogram, such as *hat*, *mat*, and *bat*. To vary the activity, supply the initial and final consonants and have children supply the medial vowel sound and letter, for example: c_t (/a/, *a*).

Popcorn Letters

Assign each child one or two letters of the alphabet to write. Each letter should be written on a separate sheet of drawing paper. Then provide a large bowl of popcorn, and have children glue the popcorn on the paper, following the shape of the letter.

Say the Word and Find the Letter

Place the lowercase letters of the alphabet in the pocket chart. Then say a sound—for example, /m/. Have children say a word that begins with that sound and point to the letter in the pocket chart that makes that sound. To modify the activity, place several letters at a time in the pocket chart instead of the entire alphabet.

Create a Story

Select a pocket chart picture for any alphabet letter and invite children to make up a story about it. Write their story on sentence strips and place them in the pocket chart. Then read the story together. Highlight any words that contain the initial/medial letter and sound on which you are focusing.

Sound/Letter Hunt

Organize a scavenger hunt for hidden objects, the names of which begin with a specific sound and letter. You may want to have pairs or small groups of children search for the objects. When they find the objects, have them say each word and beginning sound, then identify the beginning letter.

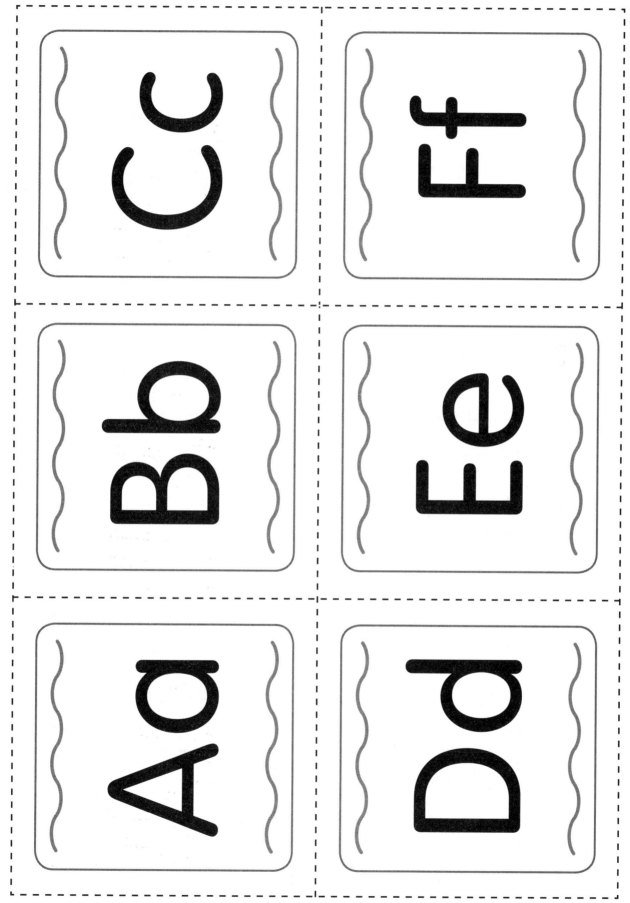

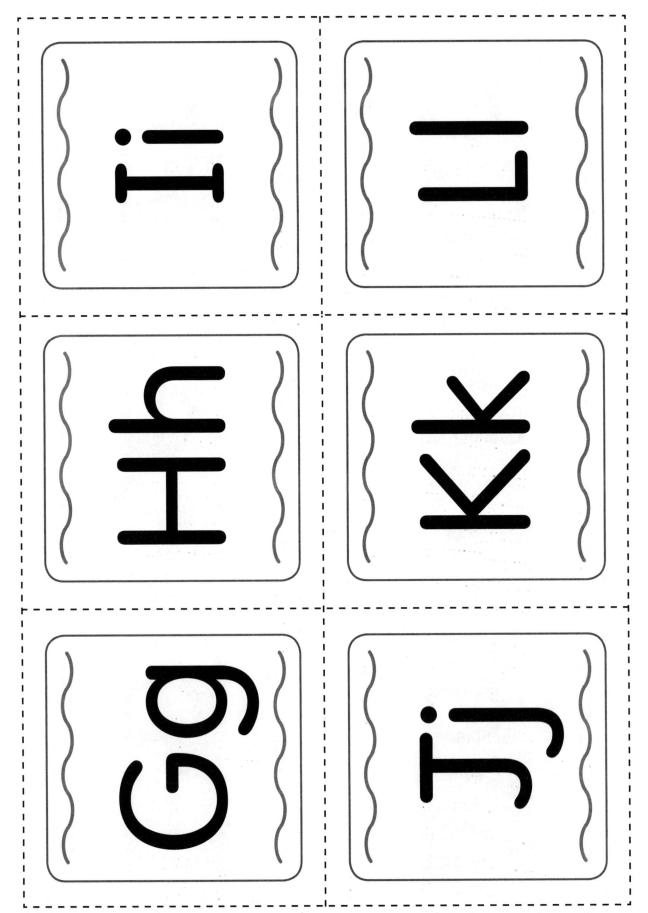

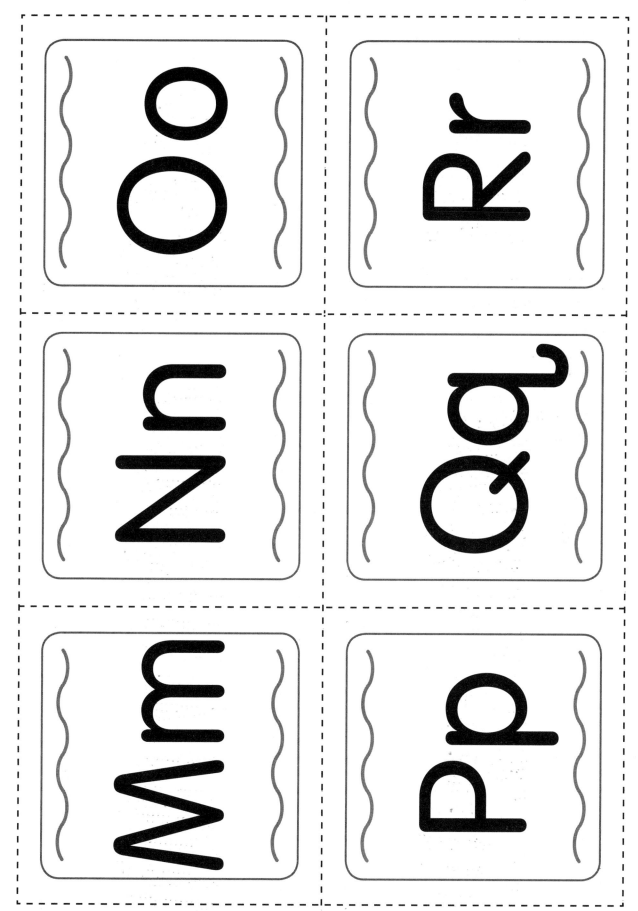

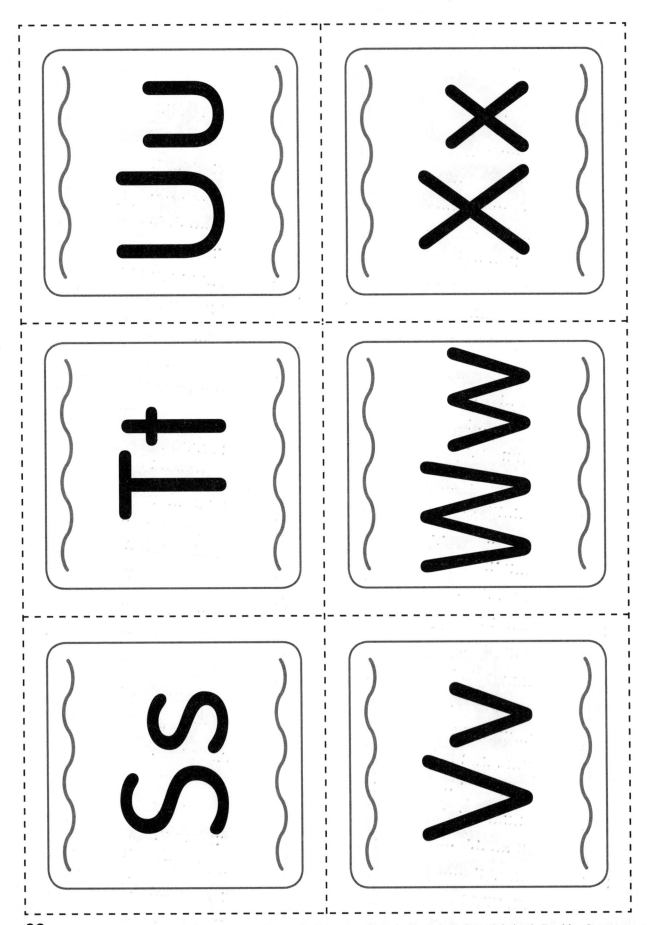

 The Big Book of Pocket Chart Poems: ABCs & 123s © 2007 by Linda B. Ross, Scholastic Teaching Resources

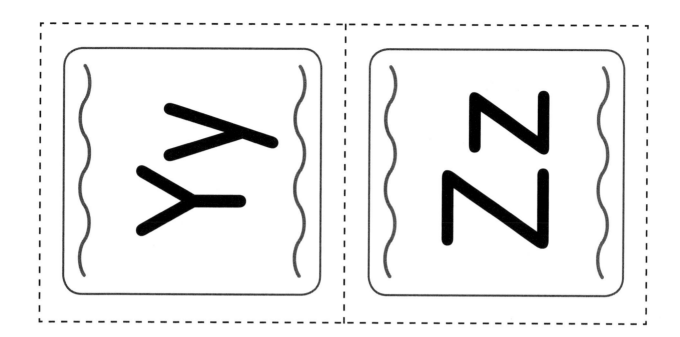

Alphabet Frame

Picture Card Template

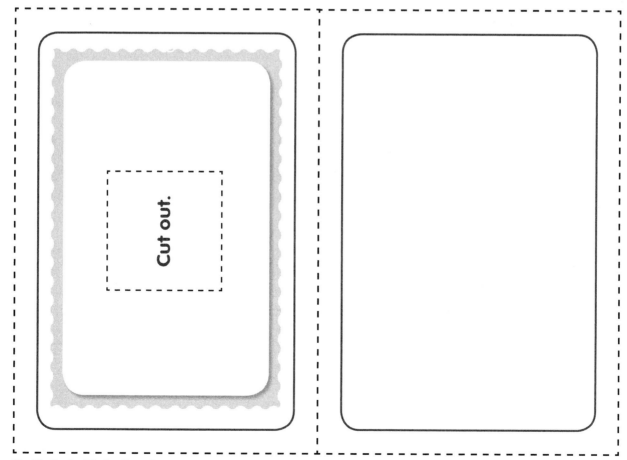

Cut out.

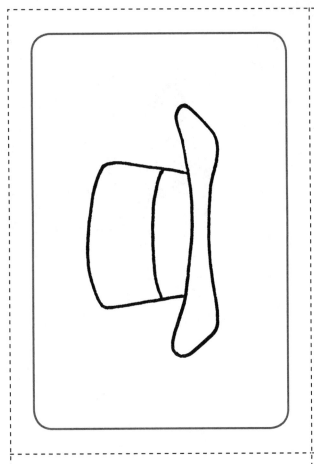

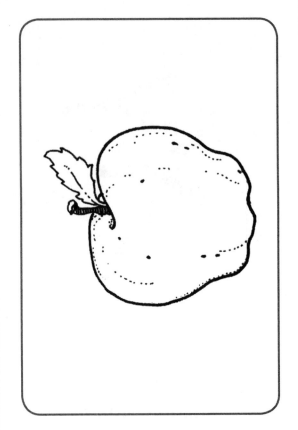

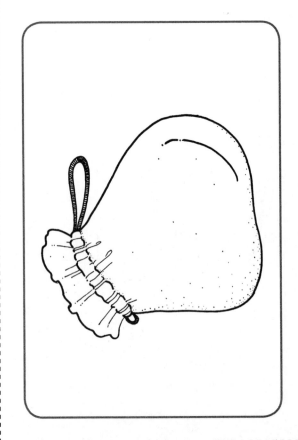

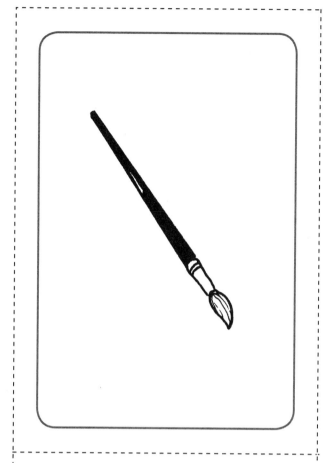

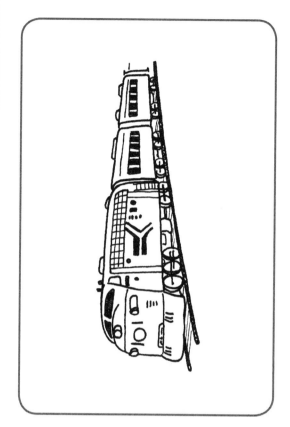

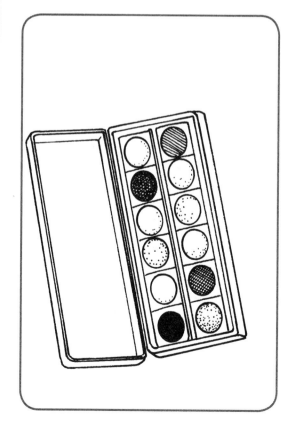

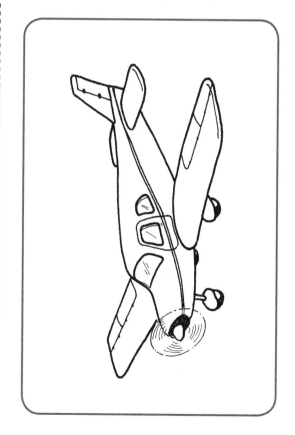

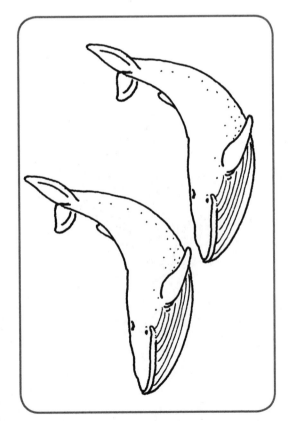

The Big Book of Pocket Chart Poems: ABCs & 123s © 2007 by Linda B. Ross, Scholastic Teaching Resources

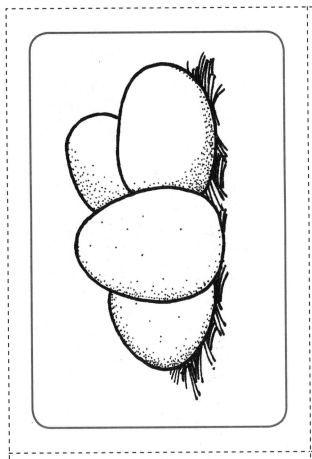

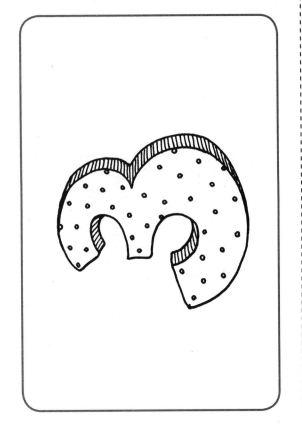

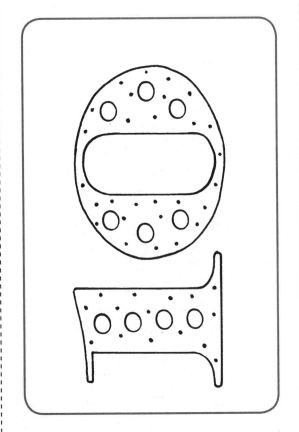

The Big Book of Pocket Chart Poems: ABCs & 123s © 2007 by Linda B. Ross, Scholastic Teaching Resources

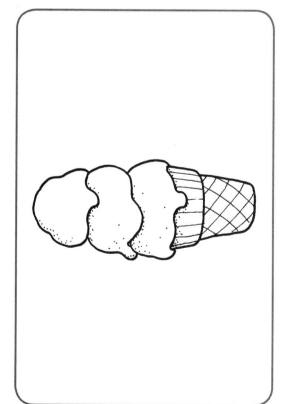

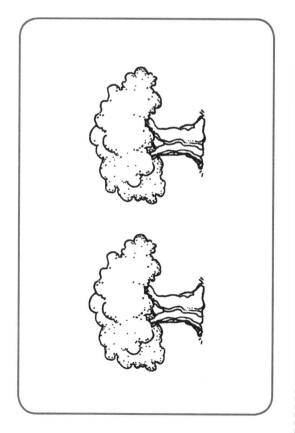

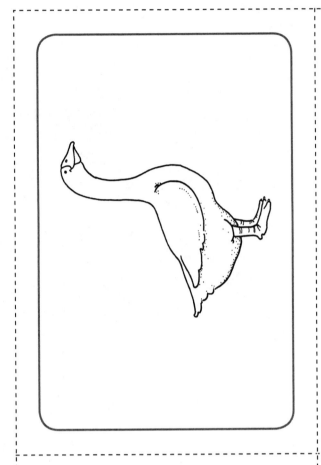

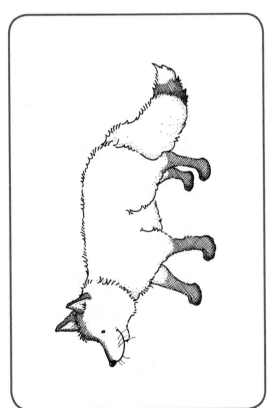

The Big Book of Pocket Chart Poems: ABCs & 123s © 2007 by Linda B. Ross, Scholastic Teaching Resources

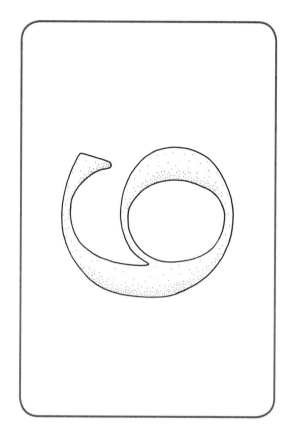

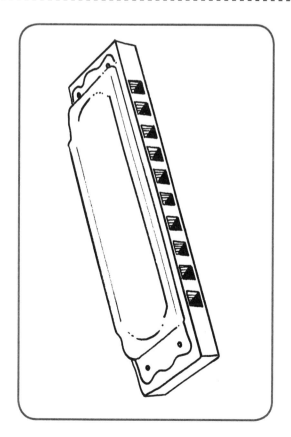

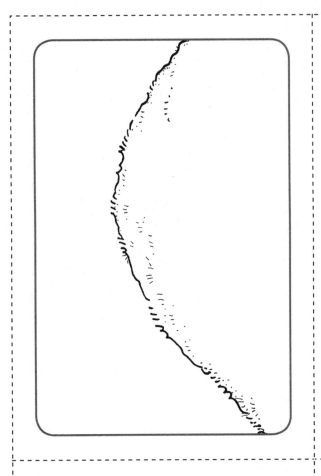

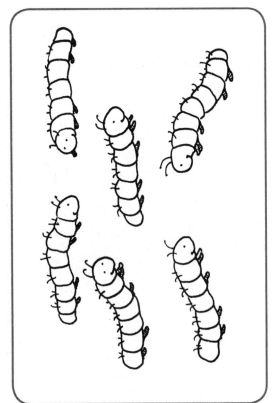

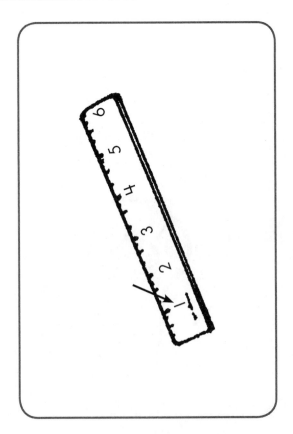

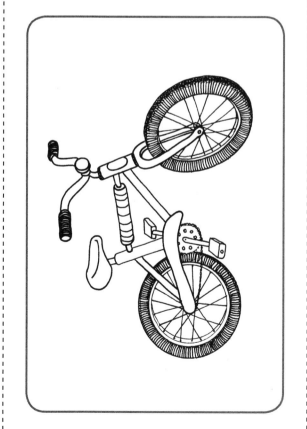

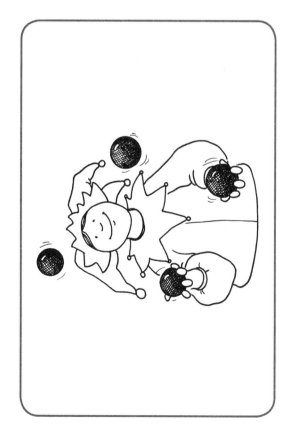

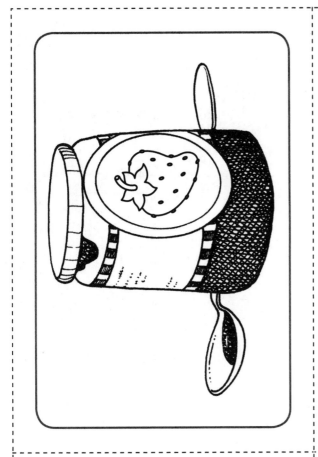

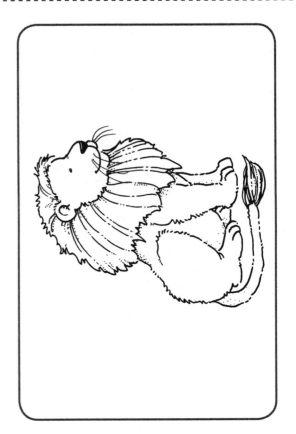

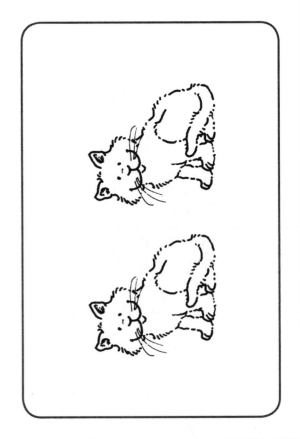

The Big Book of Pocket Chart Poems: ABCs & 123s © 2007 by Linda B. Ross, Scholastic Teaching Resources

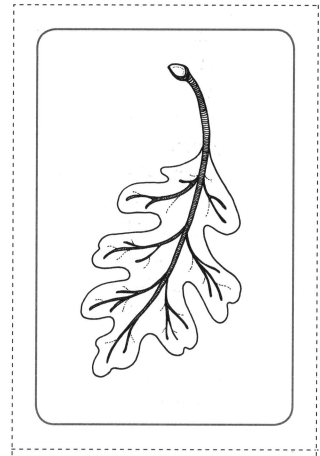

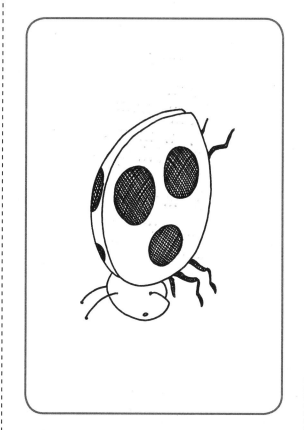

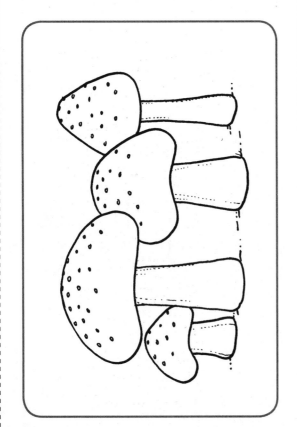

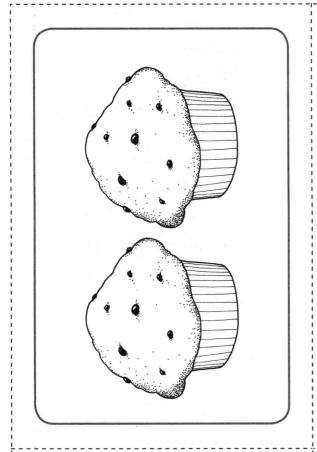

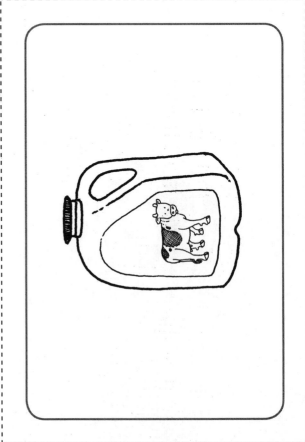

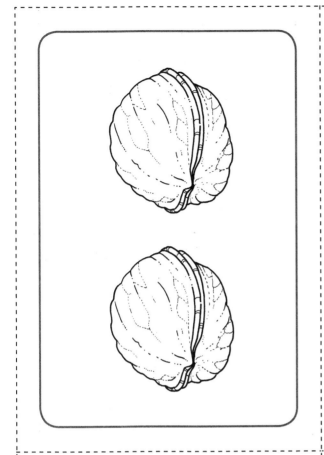

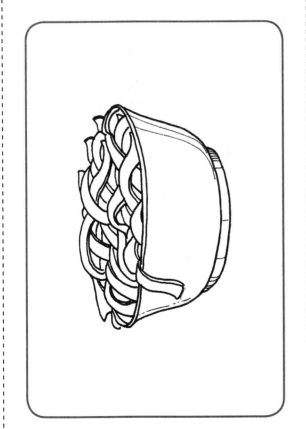

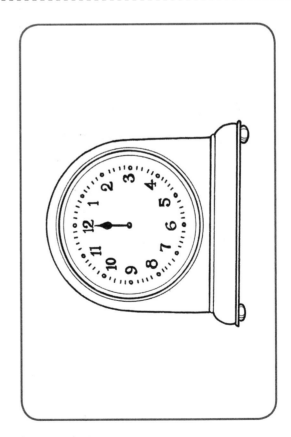

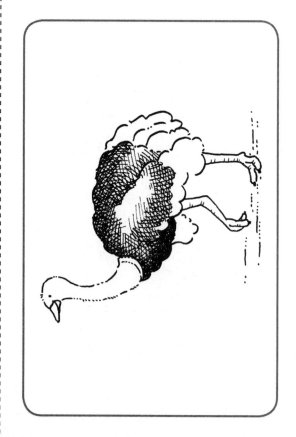

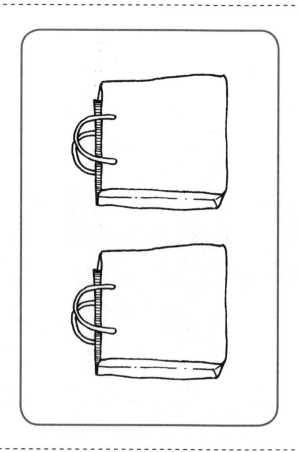

The Big Book of Pocket Chart Poems: ABCs & 123s © 2007 by Linda B. Ross, Scholastic Teaching Resources

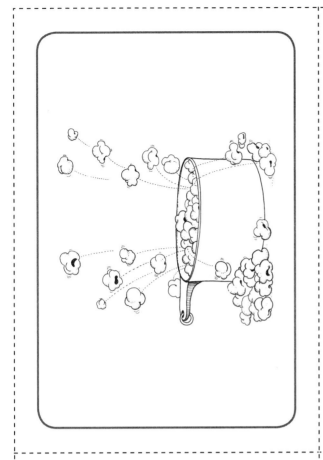

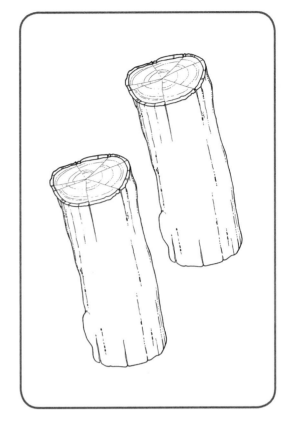

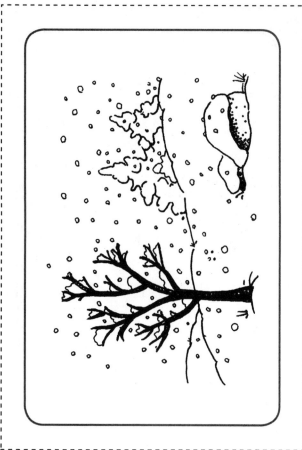

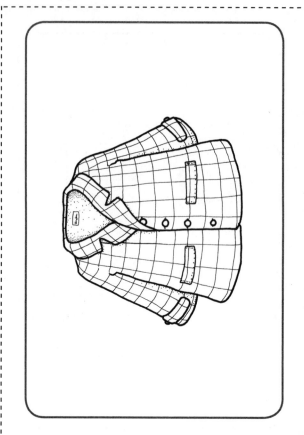

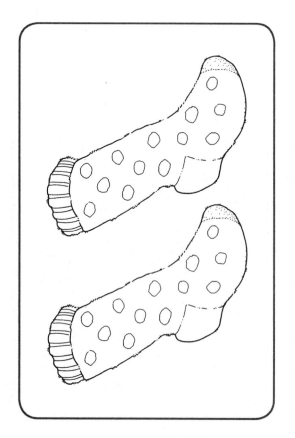

The Big Book of Pocket Chart Poems: ABCs & 123s © 2007 by Linda B. Ross, Scholastic Teaching Resources

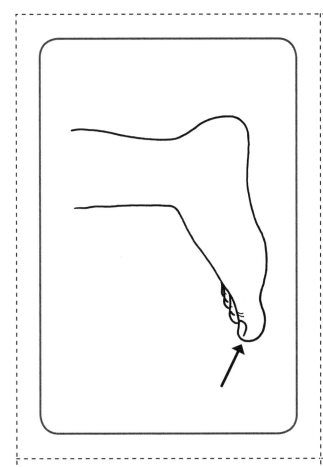

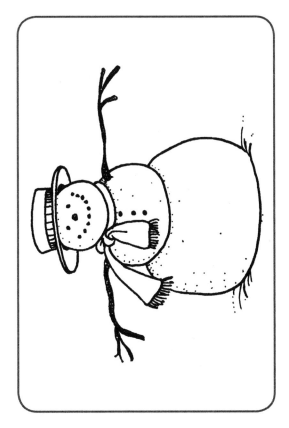

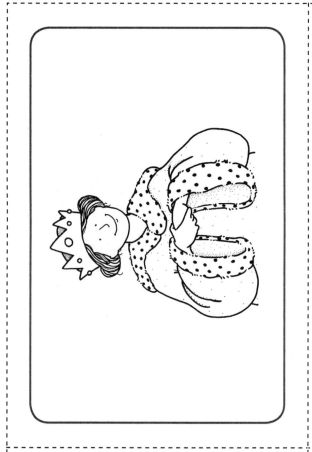

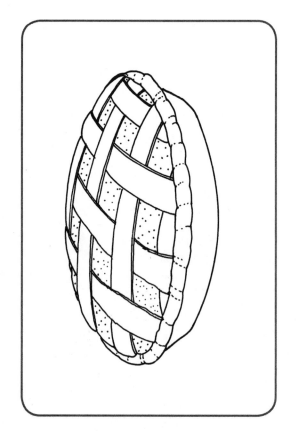

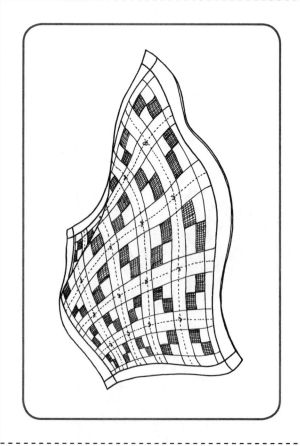

The Big Book of Pocket Chart Poems: ABCs & 123s © 2007 by Linda B. Ross, Scholastic Teaching Resources

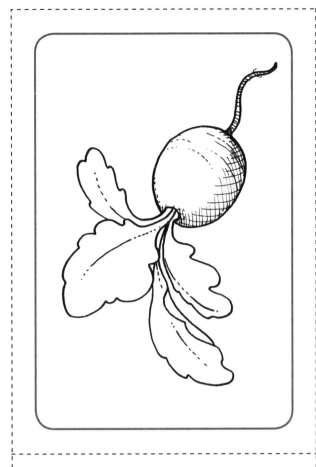

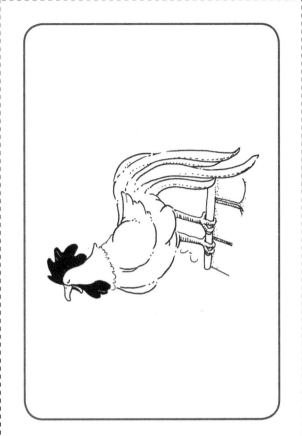

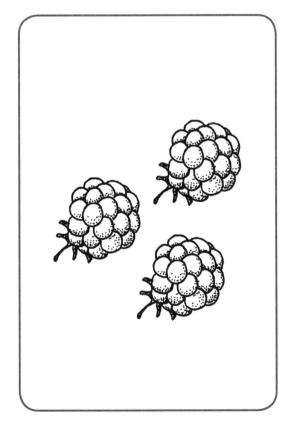

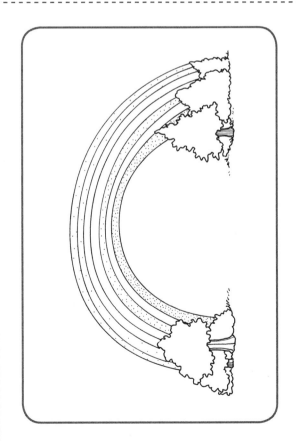

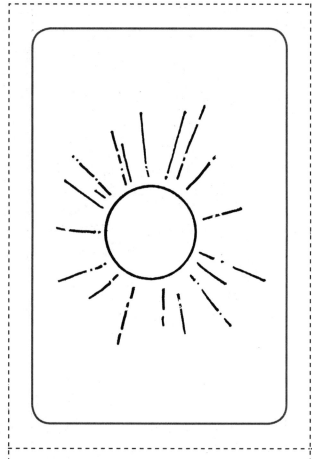

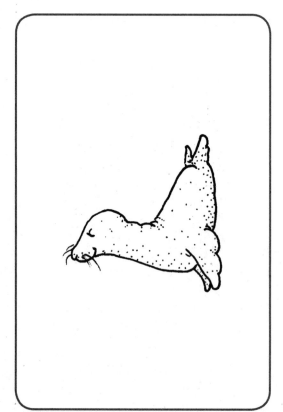

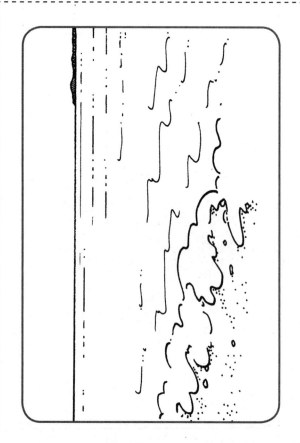

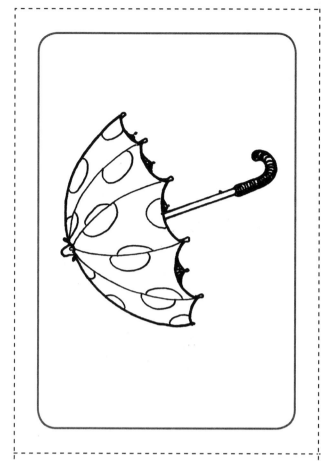

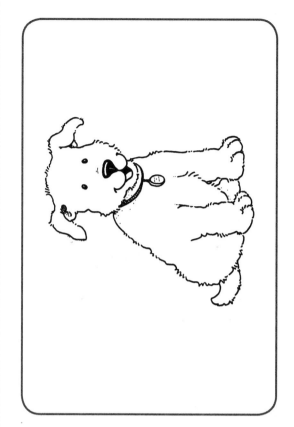

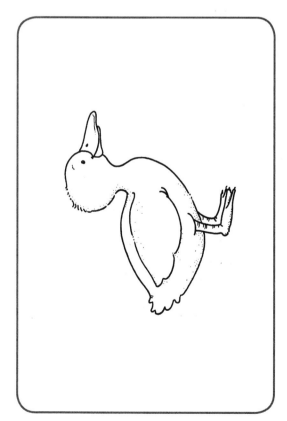

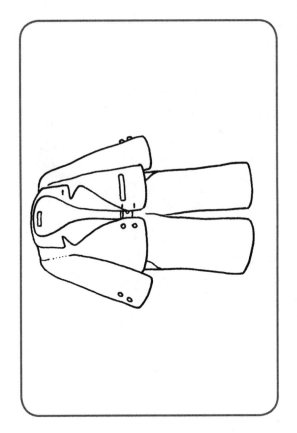

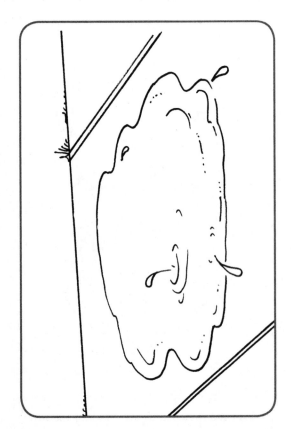

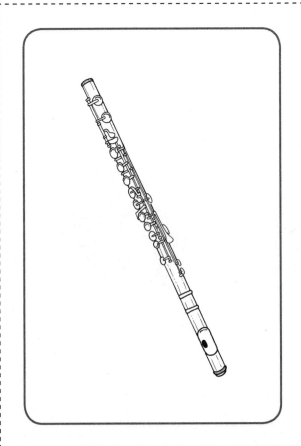

The Big Book of Pocket Chart Poems: ABCs & 123s © 2007 by Linda B. Ross, Scholastic Teaching Resources

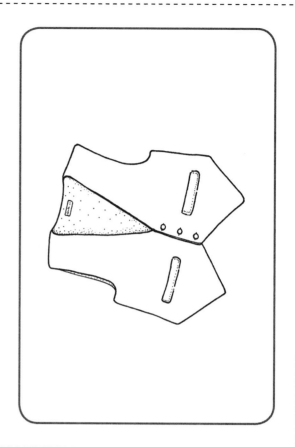

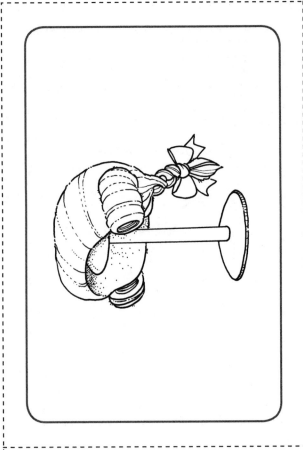

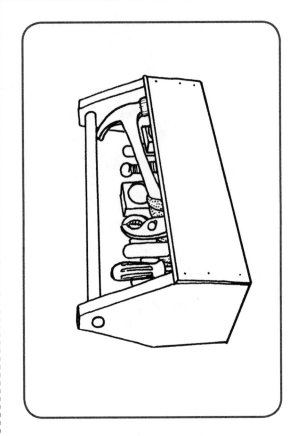

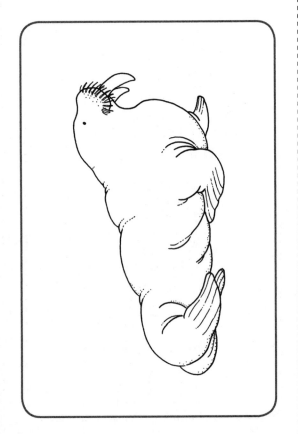

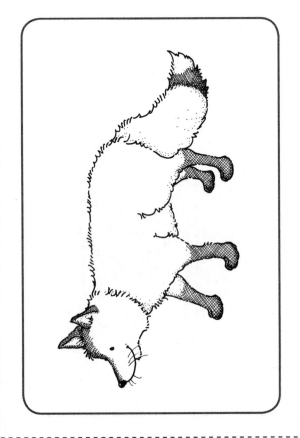

The Big Book of Pocket Chart Poems: ABCs & 123s © 2007 by Linda B. Ross, Scholastic Teaching Resources

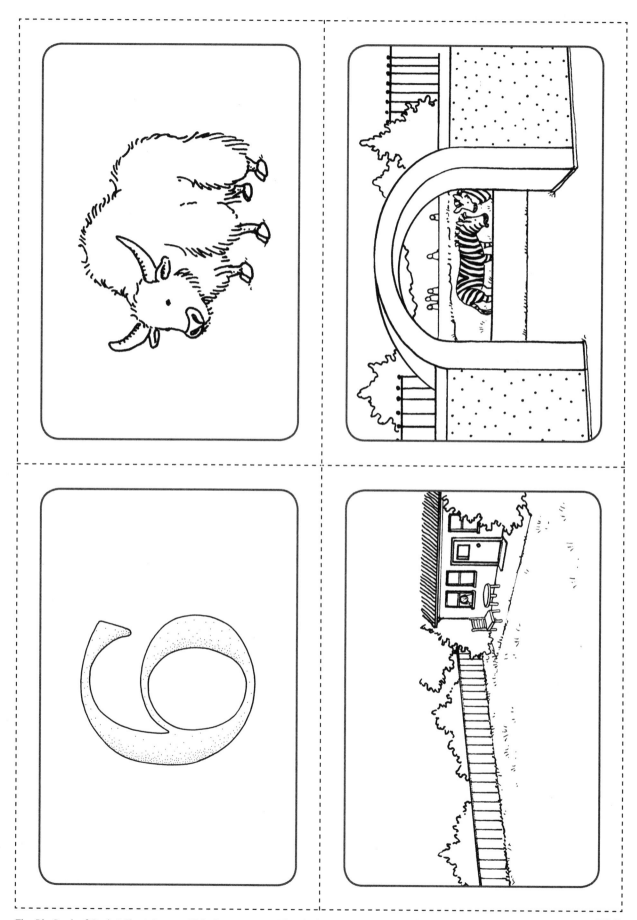

ABCs

My Book About the Letter

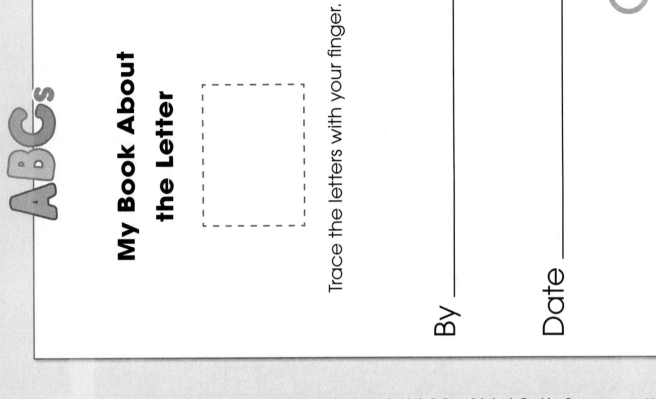

Trace the letters with your finger.

By _____

Date _____

ABCs

Trace the letter with a pencil.

Trace the letter with a pencil.

ABCs

Write the letter _____.

Write the letter _____.

③

ABCs

Write words with the letter _____.

Draw a picture on the back of this page.

④

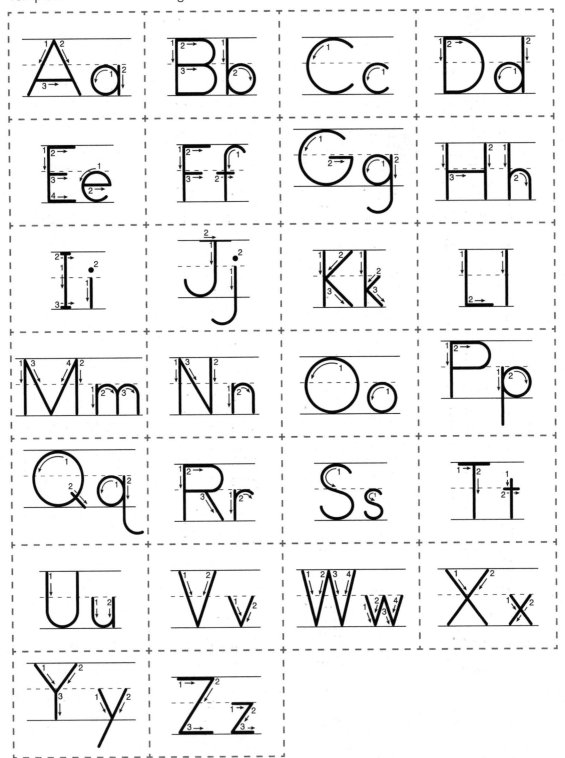

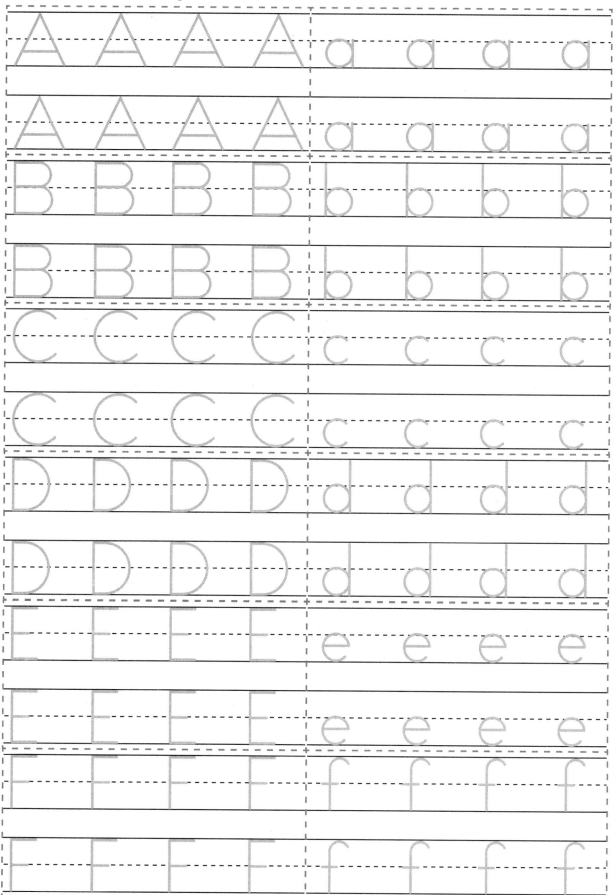

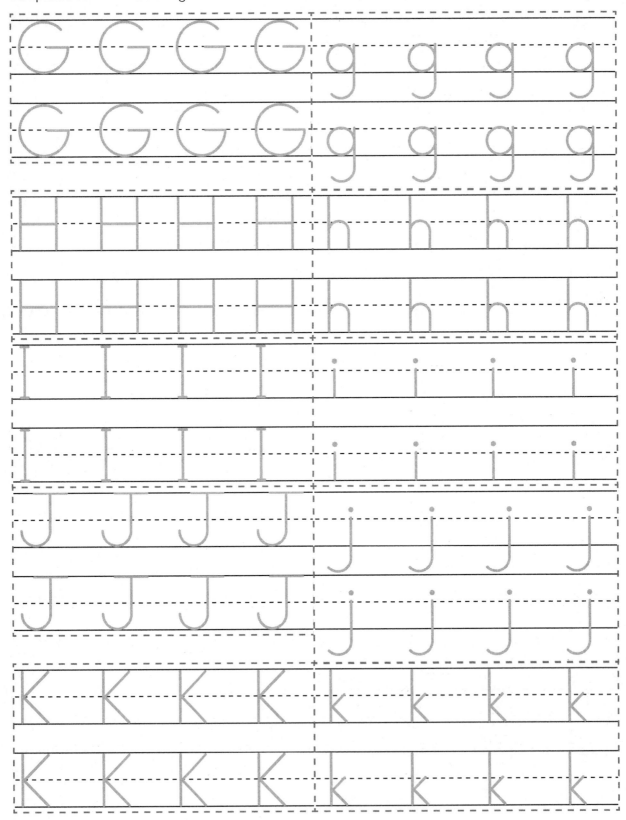

The Big Book of Pocket Chart Poems: ABCs & 123s © 2007 by Linda B. Ross, Scholastic Teaching Resources

Reproducible Letter Strips

Templates for Mini-Book Page 2

L L L L l l l l

L L L L l l l l

M M M M m m m m

M M M M m m m m

N N N N n n n n

N N N N n n n n

O O O O o o o o

O O O O o o o o

P P P P p p p p

P P P P p p p p

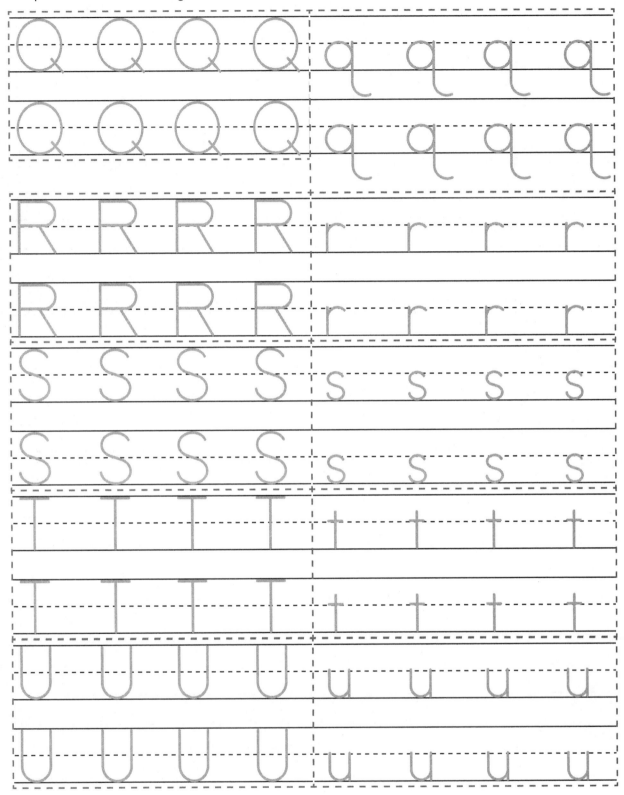

Reproducible Letter Strips

Templates for Mini-Book Page 2

V V V V v v v v

V V V V v v v v

W W W W w w w w

W W W W w w w w

X X X X x x x x

X X X X x x x x

Y Y Y Y y y y y

Y Y Y Y y y y y

Z Z Z Z z z z z

Z Z Z Z z z z z

The Number 1

1 Cat Named Nat

I have **1** cat.
His name is Nat.
He's not too thin and not too fat.
He has **1** spot
Between his eyes.
It makes him look so smart and wise.
There is **1** place
Nat loves to nap.
Can you guess where?
It's on my cap!

Materials

🌼 pocket chart

🌼 sentence strips

🌼 numeral card
(1; page 155)

🌼 picture cards
(cat, cap; page 160)

🌼 numeral frame
(page 160)

🌼 counters
(page 176)

🌼 number practice
mini-book
(pages 171–172)

🌼 numeral strips
(1; page 173)

Getting Ready

1. Copy the title and poem onto sentence strips (one line per sentence strip). Highlight the numeral 1 in lines 1, 4, and 7 (as indicated above). Place the sentence strips in order in the pocket chart.

2. Photocopy and cut apart the picture cards (cat, cap) and counters (3, plus 1 for each student for completion of the mini-book).

3. Place the picture cards and numeral card (in that order) across the top of the pocket chart. Place the counters to the side.

4. Customize the mini-book for the numeral 1, and make a class set. (See page 7 for directions.)

Teaching With the Pocket Chart Poem

1. Begin by pointing to the picture of the cat and asking: *What do you see?* (a cat) *How many cats do you see?* (one) Point to the numeral card 1 and have children name the numeral they see. Then point to the picture of the cap and ask children how many caps they see. (one)

2. Invite children to get ready to listen to a poem about one special cat. As you read the poem, emphasize the numeral 1 by pointing to it each time. Place the picture cards next to the rhyme accordingly. When you read the poem again, ask children to hold up one finger each time you say the word *one*. Let children take turns using the numeral frame to isolate each occurrence of the numeral 1 (lines 1, 4, and 7).

3. Place three counters on a table near the pocket chart. Let children take turns counting out one counter and placing it next to a line in the poem that contains the numeral 1.

4. Write the numeral 1 slowly on chart paper (or a whiteboard) to demonstrate how it is formed. Have children follow your movements by writing the numeral in the air.

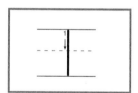

5. Give each child a copy of the mini-book and a counter. Guide children in completing pages 1–3. (See page 7 for directions.) On page 4, invite children to draw a picture of one cat playing with one toy, such as a ball. If desired, children can incorporate other representations of the number one in their pictures, such as one chair, one table, and one lamp.

6. As an extension, introduce children to the word *one*. Write the word on a sentence strip, and trim to size. Add the word card to the pocket chart. Read the word together. Then have children match the word *one* to the numeral 1 in the poem and to the corresponding number of counters. Allow time over the next few days for children to revisit the poem and manipulatives.

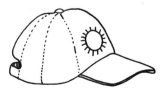

The Number 2

2 of a Kind

I have **2** eyes that help me see.
I'm glad that they belong to me.
I have **2** ears that help me hear
A whisper or a happy cheer.
I have **2** hands that do so much.
They write and catch and like to touch.
I have **2** feet that help me run,
And hop and skip and jump—what fun!

Materials

- pocket chart
- sentence strips
- numeral card
  (2; page 155)
- picture cards
  (eyes, ears, hands,
  feet; page 160)
- numeral frame
  (page 160)
- counters
  (page 176)
- number practice
  mini-book
  (pages 171–172)
- numeral strips
  (2; page 173)

Getting Ready

1. Copy the title and poem onto sentence strips (one line per sentence strip). Highlight the numeral 2 in the title and in lines 1, 3, 5, and 7 (as indicated above). Place the sentence strips in order in the pocket chart.

2. Photocopy and cut apart the picture cards (eyes, ears, hands, feet) and counters (8, plus 2 for each student for completion of the mini-book).

3. Place the picture cards and numeral card (in that order) across the top of the pocket chart. Place the counters to the side.

4. Customize the mini-book for the numeral 2, and make a class set. (See page 7 for directions.)

Teaching With the Pocket Chart Poem

1. Begin by asking: *How many eyes do you have?* Point to the numeral card 2 and have children identify it. Then point to each picture and have children tell what they see (two eyes, two ears, two hands, two feet).

2. Invite children to get ready to listen to a poem about the number two. As you read the poem, emphasize the numeral 2 by pointing to it each time. Place the picture cards next to the rhyme accordingly. When you read the poem a second time, ask children to hold up two fingers each time you say *two*. Then invite children to take turns using the numeral frame to isolate the numeral 2 each time it appears in the poem (lines 1, 3, 5, and 7).

3. Place eight counters on a table near the pocket chart. Ask a child to count out two counters and place them next to a line in the poem that contains the numeral 2. Repeat for the other lines in the poem with the numeral 2.

4. Write the numeral 2 slowly on chart paper (or a whiteboard) to demonstrate how it is formed. Have children follow your movements by using their finger to write the numeral on their palm.

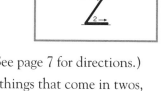

5. Give each child a copy of the mini-book and a set of counters. Guide children in completing pages 1–3. (See page 7 for directions.) On page 4, invite children to draw a picture of other things that come in twos, such as two slices of bread for a sandwich, two wheels on a bike, or two wings on a bird.

6. As an extension, introduce children to the word *two*. Write the word on a sentence strip and trim to size. Add the word card to the pocket chart. Read the word together. Then have children match the word *two* to the numeral 2 in the poem and to the corresponding number of counters. Allow time over the next few days for children to revisit the poem and manipulatives.

The Number 3

Stories About 3

There are wonderful stories
For you and for me
That like to use
The number **3**.
There's the **3** little pigs,
And the **3** bears, too.
It's fun to find out
What **3** animals can do!

Materials

🌸 pocket chart

🌸 sentence strips

🌸 numeral card
(3; page 155)

🌸 picture cards (pigs,
bears; page 161)

🌸 numeral frame
(page 160)

🌸 counters
(page 176)

🌸 number practice
mini-book (pages
171–172)

🌸 numeral strips
(3; page 173)

Getting Ready

1. Copy the title and poem onto sentence strips (one line per
sentence strip). Highlight the numeral 3 in the title and in
lines 4, 5, 6, and 8 (as indicated above). Place the sentence
strips in order in the pocket chart.

2. Photocopy and cut apart the picture cards (pigs, bears) and
counters (12, plus 3 for each student for completion of the
mini-book).

3. Place the picture cards and numeral card (in
that order) across the top of the pocket chart.
Place the counters to the side.

4. Customize the mini-book for the numeral
3, and make a class set. (See page 7
for directions.)

Teaching With the Pocket Chart Poem

1. Begin by pointing to the pictures of the pigs. Ask: *How many pigs do you see?* Have children count the pigs, and then remind them of the story. Point to the numeral card 3 and have children identify it. Invite children to count bears in the remaining picture cards (three).

2. Invite children to get ready to listen to a poem about the number three. As you read the poem, emphasize the numeral 3 by pointing to it each time. Place the picture cards next to the rhyme accordingly. When you read it again, ask children to hold up three fingers each time you say *three*. Then invite children to take turns using the numeral frame to isolate the numeral 3 each time it appears in the poem (lines 4, 5, 6, and 8).

3. Place 12 counters on a table near the pocket chart. Ask a child to count out three counters and place them next to a line in the poem that has the numeral 3. Repeat for the other lines in the poem with the numeral 3.

4. Write the numeral 3 slowly on chart paper (or a whiteboard) to show how it is formed. Then ask three children to come to the chart paper (or whiteboard) and write the numeral 3. Repeat with new groups of three children until everyone has had a turn.

5. Give each child a copy of the mini-book and a set of counters. Guide children in completing pages 1–3. (See page 7 for directions.) On page 4, invite children to draw a picture of the three little pigs or the three bears. Encourage them to include other sets of three in the picture, such as houses, flowers, and birds.

6. As an extension, introduce children to the word *three*. Write the word on a sentence strip, and trim to size. Add the word card to the pocket chart, and read the word together. Then have children match the word *three* to the numeral 3 in the poem and to the corresponding number of counters. Allow time over the next few days for children to revisit the poem and manipulatives.

The Number 4

4 Funny Monkeys

4 funny monkeys
Sitting in a tree.
I wave at them.
They wave at me.
I make a silly face,
Then they make one, too.
What the **4** monkeys see
Is what the **4** monkeys do!

Materials

- pocket chart
- sentence strips
- numeral card
  (4; page 155)
- picture cards (monkeys, tree; page 161)
- numeral frame
  (page 160)
- wall adhesive
- counters (page 176)
- number practice
  mini-book
  (pages 171–172)
- numeral strips
  (4; page 173)

Getting Ready

1. Copy the title and poem onto sentence strips (one line per sentence strip). Highlight the numeral 4 in the title and in lines 1, 7, and 8 (as indicated above). Place the sentence strips in order in the pocket chart.

2. Photocopy and cut apart the picture cards (monkeys, tree) and counters (12, plus 4 for each student for completion of the mini-book).

3. Place the picture cards and numeral card (in that order) across the top of the pocket chart. Place the counters to the side.

4. Customize the mini-book for the numeral 4, and make a class set. (See page 7 for directions.)

Teaching With the Pocket Chart Poem

1. Begin by pointing to the pictures of the monkeys and asking: *How many monkeys do you see?* Have children count the monkeys. Then point to the numeral card 4 and have children identify it.

2. Invite children to get ready to listen to a poem about four monkeys. As you read the poem, emphasize the numeral 4 by pointing to it each time. When you read the poem again, ask children to hold up four fingers each time you say the word *four*. Let children take turns using the numeral frame to isolate each occurrence of the numeral 4 (lines 1, 7, and 8).

3. Invite a volunteer to count the monkeys and use wall adhesive to place them in the tree. Return the tree with the monkeys to the pocket chart. For further practice, use the counters. Ask a child to count out four counters and place them next to a line in the poem that has the numeral 4. Repeat for the other lines in the poem with the numeral 4.

4. Write the numeral 4 slowly on chart paper (or a whiteboard) to demonstrate how it is formed. Have children follow your movements, taking turns and using their finger to write the numeral on a partner's back.

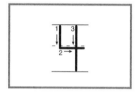

5. Give each child a copy of the mini-book and a set of counters. Guide children in completing pages 1–3. (See page 7 for directions.) On page 4, invite children to draw a picture of four monkeys doing something funny. Encourage them to include other sets of four in the picture, such as trees, lion cubs, and giraffes.

6. As an extension, introduce children to the word *four*. Write the word on a sentence strip, and trim to size. Add the word card to the pocket chart. Read the word together. Then have children match the word *four* to the numeral 4 in the poem and to the corresponding number of counters. Allow time over the next few days for children to revisit the poem and manipulatives.

The Number 5

5 Little Chicks

5 little chicks live on a farm.

Mama Hen keeps them safe from harm.

5 little chicks go off to play.

Mama Hen says, "Don't wander away!"

5 little chicks climb a big haystack.

Mama Hen brings them safely back!

Materials

🌼 pocket chart

🌼 sentence strips

🌼 numeral card
(5; page 155)

🌼 picture cards (chicks, haystack, hen; page 162)

🌼 numeral frame
(page 160)

🌼 wall adhesive

🌼 counters
(page 176)

🌼 number practice mini-book (pages 171–172)

🌼 numeral strips
(5; page 173)

Getting Ready

1. Copy the title and poem onto sentence strips (one line per sentence strip). Highlight the numeral 5 in the title and in lines 1, 3, and 5 (as indicated above). Place the sentence strips in order in the pocket chart.

2. Photocopy and cut apart the picture cards (chicks, haystack, hen) and counters (15, plus 5 for each student for completion of the mini-book).

3. Place the picture cards and numeral card (in that order) across the top of the pocket chart. Place the counters to the side.

4. Customize the mini-book for the numeral 5, and make a class set. (See page 7 for directions.)

Teaching With the Pocket Chart Poem

1. Begin by pointing to the pictures of the chicks and asking: *How many chicks do you see?* Have children count the chicks. Then point to the numeral card 5 and have children identify it.

2. Invite children to get ready to listen to a poem about five little chicks. As you read the poem, emphasize the numeral 5 by pointing to it each time. When you read the poem again, ask children to hold up five fingers each time you say the word *five*. Let children take turns using the numeral frame to isolate each occurrence of the numeral 5 (lines 1, 3, and 5).

3. Invite a volunteer to count the chicks and use wall adhesive to place them on the haystack. Affix the hen next to the haystack to complete the scene. Return the picture cards (scene intact) to the pocket chart. For further practice, use the counters. Ask a child to count out five counters and place them next to a line in the poem that has the numeral 5. Repeat for the other lines in the poem with the numeral 5.

4. Write the numeral 5 slowly on chart paper (or a whiteboard) to demonstrate how it is formed. Have children follow your movements by writing the numeral in the air.

5. Give each child a copy of the mini-book and a set of counters. Guide children in completing pages 1–3. (See page 7 for directions.) On page 4, invite children to draw a picture of five little chicks taking a walk with Mama Hen. Encourage children to include other sets of five in the picture, such as cows, pigs, and goats.

6. As an extension, introduce children to the word *five*. Write the word on a sentence strip and trim to size. Add the word card to the pocket chart. Read the word together. Then have children match the word *five* to the numeral 5 in the poem and to the corresponding number of counters. Allow time over the next few days for children to revisit the poem and manipulatives.

The Number 6

6 Little Ladybugs

6 little ladybugs wearing red and black,

With **6** little spots upon your back.

6 little ladybugs walking in a line,

Tell me why you're dressed so fine.

Dear little ladybugs, don't fly away,

In my garden you must stay!

Materials

✿ pocket chart

✿ sentence strips

✿ numeral card
(6; page 155)

✿ picture cards
(ladybug, spots;
page 162)

✿ numeral frame
(page 160)

✿ wall adhesive

✿ counters
(page 176)

✿ number practice
mini-book
(pages 171–172)

✿ numeral strips
(6; page 173)

Getting Ready

1. Copy the title and poem onto sentence strips (one line per sentence strip). Highlight the numeral 6 in the title and in lines 1, 2, and 3 (as indicated above). Place the sentence strips in order in the pocket chart.

2. Photocopy and cut apart the picture cards (making 6 copies of the ladybug card and a total of 36 spots) and counters (18, plus 6 for each student for completion of the mini-book).

3. Place the picture cards and numeral card (in that order) across the top of the pocket chart. Place the counters to the side.

4. Customize the mini-book for the numeral 6, and make a class set. (See page 7 for directions.)

The Big Book of Pocket Chart Poems: ABCs & 123s

Teaching With the Pocket Chart Poem

1. Begin by pointing to the ladybugs on the picture cards and asking: *How many ladybugs do you see?* Have children count the ladybugs aloud together. Then point to the numeral card 6 and have children identify it. Ask volunteers to point to and count other things they see (spots). Explain that children will be using the spots to complete each ladybug.

2. Tell children that they are going to listen to a poem about six ladybugs. As you read the poem, emphasize the numeral 6 by pointing to it each time. When you read the poem again, ask children to hold up six fingers each time you say the word *six*. Let children take turns using the numeral frame to isolate each occurrence of the numeral 6 (lines 1, 2, and 3).

3. Have children take turns counting out six spots for each ladybug. Have them use wall adhesive to affix the spots to the ladybugs, and then return the ladybugs to the pocket chart. For further practice, use the counters. Ask a child to count out six counters and place them next to a line in the poem that has the numeral 6. Repeat for the other lines in the poem with the numeral 6.

4. Write the numeral 6 slowly on chart paper (or a whiteboard) to demonstrate how it is formed. Have children follow your movements by using their finger to write the numeral on their palm.

5. Give each child a copy of the mini-book and a set of counters. Guide children in completing pages 1–3. (See page 7 for directions.) On page 4, invite children to draw a picture of six ladybugs in the garden. Encourage children to include other sets of six in the picture, such as flowers, bees, and birds.

6. As an extension, introduce children to the word *six*. Write the word on a sentence strip, and trim to size. Add the word card to the pocket chart. Read the word together. Then have children match the word *six* to the numeral 6 in the poem and to the corresponding number of counters. Allow time over the next few days for children to revisit the poem and manipulatives.

The Number 7

7 Diving Dolphins

7 dolphins in the sea,
Putting on a show for me!
Diving, leaping in the blue,
That's what **7** dolphins do!
7 dolphins laugh and play,
Talking in their dolphin way.
Can I come and play with you?
Let me be a dolphin too!

Materials

🌀 pocket chart

🌀 sentence strips

🌀 numeral card
(7; page 156)

🌀 picture cards (dolphins,
sea; page 163)

🌀 numeral frame
(page 160)

🌀 counters
(page 176)

🌀 number practice
mini-book
(pages 171–172)

🌀 numeral strips
(7; pages 173–174)

Getting Ready

1. Copy the title and poem onto sentence strips (one line per sentence strip). Highlight the numeral 7 in the title and in lines 1, 4, and 5 (as indicated above). Place the sentence strips in order in the pocket chart.

2. Photocopy and cut apart the picture cards (dolphins, sea) and counters (21, plus 7 for each student for completion of the mini-book).

3. Place the picture cards and numeral card (in that order) across the top of the pocket chart. Place the counters to the side.

4. Customize the mini-book for the numeral 7, and make a class set. (See page 7 for directions.)

Teaching With the Pocket Chart Poem

1. Begin by pointing to the picture of the dolphins and asking: *How many dolphins do you see?* Have children count the dolphins aloud together. Then point to the numeral card 7 and have children identify it. Invite children to tell what they see in the picture of the sea. Ask: *Do you see seven of something?* (sailboats, shells)

2. Invite children to get ready to listen to a poem about seven dolphins. As you read the poem, emphasize the numeral 7 by pointing to it each time. Place the picture cards next to the rhyme accordingly. When you read the poem again, ask children to hold up seven fingers each time you say the word *seven*. Let children take turns using the numeral frame to isolate each occurrence of the numeral 7 (lines 1, 4, and 5).

3. Place 21 counters on a table near the pocket chart. Ask a child to count out seven counters and place them next to a line in the poem that has the numeral 7. Repeat for the other lines in the poem with the numeral 7. (You may also wish to cut apart the dolphins on the picture card and enlarge the sea picture card, and then have children use wall adhesive to place the dolphins in the scene, counting to seven as they do so.)

4. Write the numeral 7 slowly on chart paper (or a whiteboard) to demonstrate how it is formed. Have children follow your movements by writing the numeral in the air.

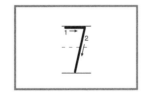

5. Give each child a copy of the mini-book and a set of counters. Guide children in completing pages 1–3. (See page 7 for directions.) On page 4, invite children to draw a picture of themselves playing with seven dolphins. Encourage them to include other sets of seven in the picture, such as clouds, boats, and birds.

6. As an extension, introduce children to the word *seven*. Write the word on a sentence strip, and trim to size. Add the word card to the pocket chart. Read the word together. Then have children match the word *seven* to the numeral 7 in the poem and to the corresponding number of counters. Allow time over the next few days for children to revisit the poem and manipulatives

The Number 8

8 Ducks Quacking

8 ducks quacking on a lake,
What a noisy group they make!
8 ducks quacking loud and clear,
Everyone around can hear!
8 ducks quacking on a lake,
I took a nap—now I'm awake!

Materials

🌸 pocket chart

🌸 sentence strips

🌸 numeral card
(8; page 156)

🌸 picture cards (ducks,
lake; page 163)

🌸 numeral frame
(page 160)

🌸 counters
(page 176)

🌸 number practice
mini-book
(pages 171–172)

🌸 numeral strips
(8; pages 173–174)

Getting Ready

1. Copy the title and poem onto sentence strips (one line per sentence strip). Highlight the numeral 8 in the title and in lines 1, 3, and 5 (as indicated above). Place the sentence strips in order in the pocket chart.

2. Photocopy and cut apart the picture cards (ducks, lake) and counters (24, plus 8 for each student for completion of the mini-book).

3. Place the picture cards and numeral card (in that order) across the top of the pocket chart. Place the counters to the side.

4. Customize the mini-book for the numeral 8, and make a class set. (See page 7 for directions.)

Teaching With the Pocket Chart Poem

1. Begin by pointing to the picture of the ducks and asking: *How many ducks do you see?* Have children count the ducks aloud together. Then point to the numeral card 8 and have children identify it. Ask volunteers to point to and count things in the picture card for lake that show eight (trees, lily pads, birds, bugs).

2. Invite children to get ready to listen to a poem about eight ducks. As you read the poem, emphasize the numeral 8 by pointing to it each time. Place the picture cards next to the rhyme accordingly. When you read the poem again, ask children to hold up eight fingers each time you say the word *eight*. Let children take turns using the numeral frame to isolate each occurrence of the numeral 8 (lines 1, 3, and 5).

3. Place 24 counters on a table near the pocket chart. Ask a child to count out eight counters and place them next to a line in the poem that has the numeral 8. Repeat for the other lines in the poem with the numeral 8. (You may also wish to cut apart the ducks on the picture card and enlarge the lake picture card, and then have children use wall adhesive to place the ducks in the lake, counting to eight as they do so.)

4. Write the numeral 8 slowly on chart paper (or a whiteboard) to demonstrate how it is formed. Have children follow your movements by taking turns and using their finger to write the numeral on a partner's back.

5. Give each child a copy of the mini-book and a set of counters. Guide children in completing pages 1–3. (See page 7 for directions.) On page 4, invite children to draw a picture of eight ducks swimming in a row. Encourage them to include other sets of eight in the picture, such as butterflies, frogs, and lily pads.

6. As an extension, introduce children to the word *eight*. Write the word on a sentence strip, and trim to size. Add the word card to the pocket chart. Read the word together. Then have children match the word *eight* to the numeral 8 in the poem and to the corresponding number of counters. Allow time over the next few days for children to revisit the poem and manipulatives.

The Number 9

9 Kites Flying

9 kites flying in the sky.
See the colors floating by.
9 kites dancing in the air.
People stop to point and stare.
9 kites flying over trees,
Kite tails wagging in the breeze.

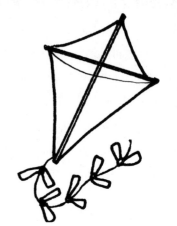

Materials

- pocket chart
- sentence strips
- numeral card
  (9; page 156)
- picture cards
  (kites, sky/trees;
  page 164)
- numeral frame
  (page 160)
- counters
  (page 176)
- number practice
  mini-book
  (pages 171–172)
- numeral strips
  (9; pages 173–174)

Getting Ready

1. Copy the title and poem onto sentence strips (one line per sentence strip). Highlight the numeral 9 in the title and in lines 1, 3, and 5 (as indicated above). Place the sentence strips in order in the pocket chart.

2. Photocopy and cut apart the picture cards (kites, sky/trees) and counters (27, plus 9 for each student for completion of the mini-book).

3. Place the picture cards and numeral card (in that order) across the top of the pocket chart. Place the counters to the side.

4. Customize the mini-book for the numeral 9, and make a class set. (See page 7 for directions.)

Teaching With the Pocket Chart Poem

1. Begin by pointing to the picture of the kites and asking: *How many kites do you see?* Have children count the kites aloud together. Then point to the numeral card 9 and have children identify it. Invite children to look at the picture of the sky/trees. Can they find sets of nine in this picture? (birds, butterflies, flowers)

2. Invite children to get ready to listen to a poem about nine kites. As you read the poem, emphasize the numeral 9 by pointing to it each time. Place the picture cards next to the rhyme accordingly. When you read the poem again, ask children to hold up nine fingers each time you say the word *nine*. Let children take turns using the numeral frame to isolate each occurrence of the numeral 9 (lines 1, 3, and 5).

3. Place 27 counters on a table near the pocket chart. Ask a child to count out nine counters and place them next to a line in the poem that has the numeral 9. Repeat for the other lines in the poem with the numeral 9. (You may also wish to cut apart the kites in the picture card and enlarge the sky/tree picture, and then have children use wall adhesive to place the kites in the sky, counting to nine as they do so.)

4. Write the numeral 9 slowly on chart paper (or a whiteboard) to demonstrate how it is formed. Have children follow your movements by using their finger to write the numeral on their palm.

5. Give each child a copy of the mini-book and a set of counters. Guide children in completing pages 1–3. (See page 7 for directions.) On page 4, invite children to draw a picture of nine kites in the air. Encourage them to include other sets of nine in the picture, such as clouds, birds, and trees.

6. As an extension, introduce children to the word *nine*. Write the word on a sentence strip, and trim to size. Add the word card to the pocket chart. Read the word together. Then have children match the word *nine* to the numeral 9 in the poem and to the corresponding number of counters. Allow time over the next few days for children to revisit the poem and manipulatives.

The Number 10

10 Turtles Racing

Each summer in a special place,
10 turtles have a turtle race.
The other animals gather there,
As if it were a country fair,
To watch **10** turtles creep and crawl,
And cheer the fastest one of all!

Materials

- pocket chart
- sentence strips
- numeral card (10; page 156)
- picture cards (turtles, rabbits, bears; page 165)
- numeral frame (page 160)
- counters (page 176)
- number practice mini-book (pages 171–172)
- numeral strips (10; pages 173–174)

Getting Ready

1. Copy the title and poem onto sentence strips (one line per sentence strip). Highlight the numeral 10 in the title and in lines 2 and 5 (as indicated above). Place the sentence strips in order in the pocket chart.

2. Photocopy and cut apart the picture cards (turtles, rabbits, bears) and counters (20, plus 10 for each student for completion of the mini-book).

3. Place the picture cards and numeral card (in that order) across the top of the pocket chart. Place the counters to the side.

4. Customize the mini-book for the numeral 10, and make a class set. (See page 7 for directions.)

Teaching With the Pocket Chart Poem

1. Begin by pointing to the picture of the turtles and asking: *How many turtles are there?* Have children count the turtles aloud together. Then point to the numeral card 10 and have children identify it. Ask volunteers to point to and count the other groups of animals in the pictures (10 rabbits, 10 bears).

2. Invite children to get ready to listen to a poem about ten turtles. As you read the poem, emphasize the numeral 10 by pointing to it each time. Place the picture cards next to the rhyme accordingly. When you read the poem again, ask children to hold up ten fingers each time you say the word *ten*. Let children take turns using the numeral frame to isolate each occurrence of the numeral 10 (lines 2 and 5).

3. Place 20 counters on a table near the pocket chart. Ask a child to count out 10 counters and place them next to a line in the poem that has the numeral 10. Repeat for the other line in the poem with the numeral 10.

4. Write the numeral 10 slowly on chart paper (or a whiteboard) to demonstrate how it is formed. Have children follow your movements by writing the numeral in the air.

5. Give each child a copy of the mini-book and a set of counters. Guide children in completing pages 1–3. (See page 7 for directions.) On page 4, invite children to draw a picture of ten turtles at the end of the race. Encourage them to include other sets of ten in the picture, such as trees or birds.

6. As an extension, introduce children to the word *ten*. Write the word on a sentence strip, and trim to size. Add the word card to the pocket chart. Read the word together. Then have children match the word *ten* to the numeral 10 in the poem and to the corresponding number of counters. Allow time over the next few days for children to revisit the poem and manipulatives.

The Number 11

11 Sitting Seals

11 seals sit by the sea,
Spinning balls so gracefully.
With a ball upon each nose,
What a grand and funny pose.
11 balls twirl round and round.
You can hardly hear a sound.
Soon the seals can spin no more
Because their noses are too sore!

Materials

- pocket chart
- sentence strips
- numeral card
  (11; page 156)
- picture cards
  (seals, beach balls;
  page 166)
- numeral frame
  (page 160)
- counters
  (page 176)
- number practice
  mini-book
  (pages 171–172)
- numeral strips
  (11; page 173–174)

Getting Ready

1. Copy the title and poem onto sentence strips (one line per sentence strip). Highlight the numeral 11 in the title and in lines 1 and 5 (as indicated above). Place the sentence strips in order in the pocket chart.

2. Photocopy a class set plus one extra of the numeral card. Photocopy and cut apart the picture cards (seals, beach balls) and counters (22, plus 11 for each student for completion of the mini-book).

3. Place the picture cards and a numeral card (in that order) across the top of the pocket chart. Place the counters and extra numeral cards to the side.

4. Customize the mini-book for the numeral 11, and make a class set. (See page 7 for directions.)

Teaching With the Pocket Chart Poem

1. Begin by pointing to the picture of the seals and asking: *How many seals do you see?* Have children count the seals aloud together. Then point to the numeral card 11 and have children identify it. Invite children to name and count the other group of 11 (beach balls).

2. Give each child a numeral card 11, and tell children to get ready to listen to a poem about 11 seals. As you read the poem, emphasize the numeral 11 by pointing to it each time. Place the picture cards next to the rhyme accordingly. When you read the poem again, ask children to hold up the numeral card 11 each time you say the word *eleven*. Let children take turns using the numeral frame to isolate each occurrence of the numeral 11 (lines 1 and 5).

3. Place 22 counters on a table near the pocket chart. Ask a child to count out 11 counters and place them next to a line in the poem that has the numeral 11. Repeat for the other line in the poem with the numeral 11. (You may also want to cut apart each seal and ball, and let children use wall adhesive to place a ball on each seal's nose, counting to 11 as they go.)

4. Write the numeral 11 slowly on chart paper (or a whiteboard) to demonstrate how it is formed. Have children follow your movements by using their finger to write the numeral on their palm.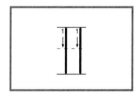

5. Give each child a copy of the mini-book and a set of counters. Guide children in completing pages 1–3. (See page 7 for directions.) On page 4, invite children to draw 11 balls. Encourage them to include other sets of 11 in the picture, such as 11 dots or other decorations on each ball.

6. As an extension, introduce children to the word *eleven*. Write the word on a sentence strip, and trim to size. Add the word card to the pocket chart. Read the word together. Then have children match the word *eleven* to the numeral 11 in the poem and to the corresponding number of counters. Allow time over the next few days for children to revisit the poem and manipulatives.

The Numbers 12 and 13

Balloon Count

My friend Jack has **12** balloons.

He bought them at the fair.

His **12** balloons are colored red.

He takes them everywhere.

My friend Jill has **13** balloons.

Her **13** balloons are blue.

And every day she says to Jack,

"I have more balloons than you!"

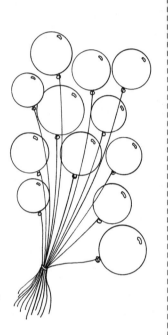

Materials

🟢 pocket chart

🟢 sentence strips

🟢 numeral cards (12 and 13; pages 156–157)

🟢 picture cards (12 balloons, 13 balloons; page 167)

🟢 numeral frame (page 160)

🟢 counters (pages 176)

🟢 number practice mini-book (pages 171–172)

🟢 numeral strips (12 and 13; pages 173–174)

Getting Ready

1. Copy the title and poem onto sentence strips (one line per sentence strip). Highlight the numerals 12 and 13 in lines 1, 3, 5, and 6 (as indicated above). Place the sentence strips in order in the pocket chart.

2. Copy a class set plus one extra of each numeral card. Photocopy and cut apart the picture cards (12 balloons, 13 balloons) and counters (50, plus 25 for each student for completion of the mini-books).

3. Place the picture cards and one of each numeral card (in that order) across the top of the pocket chart. Place the counters and extra numeral cards to the side.

4. Customize a mini-book for each numeral (12 and 13), and make a class set. (See page 7 for directions.)

Teaching With the Pocket Chart Poem

1. Begin by pointing to the picture of 12 balloons. Ask: *How many balloons are there?* Have children count the balloons aloud together. Then point to the numeral card 12 and have children identify it. Repeat the process for 13 balloons.

2. Give each child numeral cards 12 and 13, and tell children to get ready to listen to a poem about a boy who has 12 balloons and a girl who has 13 balloons. Place the picture cards next to the rhyme accordingly. As you read the poem, emphasize the numerals 12 and 13 by pointing to them each time. When you read the poem again, ask children to hold up the correct numeral card each time you say the words *twelve* and *thirteen*. Let children take turns using the numeral frame to isolate each occurrence of the numerals 12 and 13 (lines 1, 3, 5, and 6).

3. Place 50 counters on a table near the pocket chart. Ask a child to count out 12 counters and place them next to a line in the poem that has the numeral 12. Repeat for the other line in the poem with the numeral 12. Then continue with the numeral 13. Guide children to recognize that 13 is one more than 12. (Lining up the counters will help children comprehend the difference.)

4. Write the numerals 12 and 13 slowly on chart paper (or a whiteboard) to demonstrate how they are formed. Have children follow your movements by using their finger to write the numerals on a partner's back. The partner can guess which numeral it is: 12 or 13.

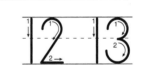

5. Give each child a copy of the mini-books and a set of counters. Guide children in completing pages 1–3 of each book. (See page 7 for directions.) On page 4 of each mini-book, invite children to draw the corresponding number of balloons. To go further, they can include other sets of 12 and 13, such as a ribbon on each balloon, or 12 or 13 stars or other shapes on or around the balloons.

6. As an extension, introduce children to the words *twelve* and *thirteen*. Write the words on a sentence strip, and trim to size. Add the word cards to the pocket chart. Read the words together. Then have children match the words *twelve* and *thirteen* to the numerals 12 and 13 in the poem and to the corresponding number of counters. Allow time over the next few days for children to revisit the poem and manipulatives.

The Numbers 14 and 15

One Summer Night

One summer night in June,
Beneath the yellow moon,
14 birds in a tree
Sing a summer song for me.
15 frogs leap around,
Making hardly any sound,
One summer night in June,
Beneath the yellow moon.

Materials

❀ pocket chart

❀ sentence strips

❀ numeral cards (14 and 15; page 157)

❀ picture cards (birds, tree/moon, frogs; pages 167–168)

❀ numeral frame (page 160)

❀ counters (page 176)

❀ number practice mini-book (pages 171–172)

❀ numeral strips (14 and 15; pages 173–174)

Getting Ready

1. Copy the title and poem onto sentence strips (one line per sentence strip). Highlight the numerals 14 and 15 in lines 3 and 5 (as indicated above). Place the sentence strips in order in the pocket chart.

2. Photocopy a class set plus one extra of each numeral card. Photocopy and cut apart the picture cards (birds, tree/moon, frogs) and counters (29, plus 29 for each student for completion of the mini-books).

3. Place the picture cards and one of each numeral card (in that order) across the top of the pocket chart. Place the counters and extra numeral cards to the side.

4. Customize a copy of the mini-book for each numeral (14 and 15), and make a class set. (See page 7 for directions.)

Teaching With the Pocket Chart Poem

1. Begin by pointing to the picture of the birds and asking: *How many birds do you see?* Have children count the birds aloud together. Then point to the numeral card 14 and have children identify it. Repeat the process for the frogs and stars in the sky and the numeral card 15.

2. Give each child numeral cards 14 and 15, and tell children to get ready to listen to a poem about 14 birds and 15 frogs. As you read the poem, emphasize the numerals 14 and 15 by pointing to them each time. Place the picture cards next to the rhyme accordingly. When you read the poem again, ask children to hold up the numeral card for 14 or 15 when you say the words *fourteen* and *fifteen*. Let children take turns using the numeral frame to isolate each occurrence of the numerals 14 and 15 (lines 3 and 5).

3. Place 29 counters on a table near the pocket chart. Ask a child to count out 14 counters and place them next to the line in the poem that has the numeral 14. Call on another child to count out 15 counters and place them next to the line that has the numeral 15. Guide children to notice that 15 is one more than 14. Lining up the counters for 14 and 15 will help children comprehend the difference. (You may also cut apart the birds and the frogs and let children use wall adhesive to place them around the tree, counting them as they go.)

4. Write the numerals 14 and 15 slowly on chart paper (or a whiteboard) to demonstrate how they are formed. Have children follow your movements by writing the numerals in the air.

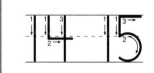

5. Give each child a copy of the mini-books and a set of counters. Guide children in completing pages 1–3. (See page 7 for directions.) On page 4 of each mini-book, invite children to draw a picture that represents the corresponding numeral. Using the poem as inspiration, they might draw 14 birds on a tree in one book, and 15 frogs jumping on the ground in the other. Encourage them to include other sets of 14 and 15 in their pictures, such as stars in the sky.

6. As an extension, introduce children to the words *fourteen* and *fifteen*. Write the words on a sentence strip, and trim to size. Add the word cards to the pocket chart and read them together. Then have children match the words *fourteen* and *fifteen* to the numerals 14 and 15 in the poem and to the corresponding number of counters. Allow time for children to revisit the poem and manipulatives.

The Numbers 16 and 17

16 Pies and 17 Cakes!

16 pies and **17** cakes,

That's what my favorite baker bakes!

17 cakes and **16** pies,

Each one is a delicious prize!

Which one do I want to choose?

There is no way I can lose!

Materials

- pocket chart
- sentence strips
- numeral cards (16 and 17; page 157)
- picture cards (pies, cakes; page 169)
- numeral frame (page 160)
- counters (page 176)
- number practice mini-book (pages 171–172)
- numeral strips (16 and 17; pages 173–174)

Getting Ready

1. Copy the title and poem onto sentence strips (one line per sentence strip). Highlight the numerals 16 and 17 in the title and in lines 1 and 3 (as indicated above). Place the sentence strips in order in the pocket chart.

2. Photocopy a class set plus one extra of the numeral cards. Photocopy and cut apart the picture cards (pies, cakes) and counters (66, plus 33 for each student for completion of the mini-books).

3. Place the picture cards and one of each numeral card (in that order) across the top of the pocket chart. Place the counters and extra numeral cards to the side.

4. Customize a copy of the mini-book for each numeral (16 and 17), and make a class set. (See page 7 for directions.)

Teaching With the Pocket Chart Poem

1. Begin by pointing to the picture of the pies and asking: *How many pies do you see?* Have children count the pies aloud together. Then point to the numeral card 16 and have children identify it. Repeat the process for the cakes and the numeral card 17.

2. Give each child numeral cards 16 and 17, and tell children to get ready to listen to a poem about 16 pies and 17 cakes. As you read the poem, emphasize the numerals 16 and 17 by pointing to them each time. Place the picture cards next to the rhyme accordingly. When you read the poem again, ask children to hold up the numeral card for 16 or 17 each time you say the word. Let children take turns using the numeral frame to isolate each occurrence of the numerals 16 and 17 (lines 1 and 3).

3. Place 66 counters on a table near the pocket chart. Ask a child to count out 16 counters and place them next to a line in the poem that has the numeral 16. Repeat for the other line in the poem with the numeral 16. Then continue with the numeral 17. Have children place each row of 17 counters below each row of 16 counters. Guide children to notice that 17 is one more than 16.

4. Write the numerals 16 and 17 slowly on chart paper (or a whiteboard) to demonstrate how they are formed. Have children follow your movements by using their finger to write the numerals on their palms.

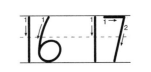

5. Give each child a copy of the mini-books and a set of counters. Guide children in completing pages 1–3. (See page 7 for directions.) On page 4 of each mini-book, invite children to draw a picture of the pies (16) and cakes (17). Encourage them to include other sets of 16 and 17 in their pictures, such as cookies and cupcakes.

6. As an extension, introduce children to the words *sixteen* and *seventeen*. Write the words on a sentence strip, and trim to size. Add the word cards to the pocket chart. Read the words together. Then have children match the words *sixteen* and *seventeen* to the numerals 16 and 17 in the poem and to the corresponding number of counters. Allow time over the next few days for children to revisit the poem and manipulatives.

The Numbers 18 and 19

Lots of Spots

I see a leopard with **18** spots.

His **18** spots are dark, round dots.

Another leopard has one spot more.

She has **19** spots for sure!

That's a lot of spots to count.

19 is a large amount!

Materials

- pocket chart
- sentence strips
- numeral cards (18 and 19; pages 157–158)
- picture cards (leopard, spots; pages 169–170)
- numeral frame (page 160)
- wall adhesive
- counters (page 176)
- number practice mini-book (pages 171–172)
- numeral strips (18 and 19; pages 173–175)

Getting Ready

1. Copy the title and poem onto sentence strips (one line per sentence strip). Highlight the numerals 18 and 19 in lines 1, 2, 4, and 6 (as indicated above). Place the sentence strips in order in the pocket chart.

2. Photocopy a class set plus one extra of the numeral cards 18 and 19. Photocopy and cut apart the picture cards (make two leopards, a set of 18 spots, and a set of 19 spots) and counters (74, plus 37 for each student for completion of the mini-books).

3. Place the picture cards and one of each numeral card (in that order) across the top of the pocket chart. Place the counters and extra numeral cards to the side.

4. Customize a copy of the mini-book for each numeral (18 and 19), and make a class set. (See page 7 for directions.)

Teaching With the Pocket Chart Poem

1. Begin by pointing to the leopard picture cards. Ask: *What do these leopards need?* Explain that children will be putting spots on each leopard. Then ask them to count each set of spots aloud together as you point to them. After counting each set of spots, point to the corresponding numeral card and have children identify it.

2. Give each child a set of numeral cards, and ask children to get ready to listen to a poem about a leopard with 18 spots and a leopard with 19 spots. As you read the poem, emphasize the numerals 18 and 19 by pointing to them each time. When you read the poem again, ask children to hold up the numeral card for 18 or 19 each time you say the word. Let children take turns using the numeral frame to isolate each occurrence of the numerals 18 and 19 (lines 1, 2, 4, and 6).

3. Remove the leopards and spots from the pocket chart. Ask a child to count out 18 spots and use wall adhesive to place them on a leopard. Repeat for the other leopard and 19 spots. Return the leopards with their spots to the pocket chart. For further practice, use the counters. Ask volunteers to count out 18 counters and place them next to the lines in the poem that have the number 18. Then continue with the number 19. Encourage children to line up the counters in each row and to recognize that 19 is one more than 18.

4. Write the numerals 18 and 19 slowly on chart paper (or a whiteboard) to demonstrate how they are formed. Have children follow your movements by writing the numerals in the air.

5. Give each child a copy of the mini-books and a set of counters. Guide children in completing pages 1–3. (See page 7 for directions.) On page 4 of each mini-book, invite children to draw a picture of another animal with either 18 or 19 spots (or stripes)—for example, a tiger, a zebra, or a giraffe.

6. As an extension, introduce children to the words *eighteen* and *nineteen*. Write the words on a sentence strip, and trim to size. Add the word cards to the pocket chart. Read the words together. Then have children match the words *eighteen* and *nineteen* to the numerals 18 and 19 in the poem and to the corresponding number of counters. Allow time over the next few days for children to revisit the poem and manipulatives.

The Number 20

How Many Apples?

20 apples on a tree,
Red and shiny as can be.
I will pick them happily,
And then take them home with me.
20 apples, my, oh my!
We can bake an apple pie,
Or two or three or even more,
Since apple pies I do adore!

Materials

- pocket chart
- sentence strips
- numeral card (20; page 158)
- picture cards (apples, tree; page 170)
- numeral frame (page 160)
- wall adhesive
- counters (page 176)
- number practice mini-book (pages 171–172)
- numeral strips (20; pages 173, 175)

Getting Ready

1. Copy the title and poem onto sentence strips (one line per sentence strip). Highlight the numeral 20 in lines 1 and 5. Place the sentence strips in order in the pocket chart.

2. Photocopy a class set plus one extra of the numeral card 20. Photocopy and cut apart the picture cards (apples, tree) and counters (40, plus 20 for each student for completion of the mini-book).

3. Place the picture cards and a numeral card (in that order) across the top of the pocket chart. Place the counters and extra numeral cards to the side.

4. Customize the mini-book for the numeral 20, and make a class set. (See page 7 for directions.)

Teaching With the Pocket Chart Poem

1. Begin by pointing to the picture of the tree and asking: *How many apples do you see on the tree?* (0) Then direct children's attention to the apple picture cards and count them aloud together. Point to the numeral card 20 and have children identify it.

2. Give each child a numeral card 20, and ask children to get ready to listen to a poem about 20 apples. As you read the poem, emphasize the numeral 20 by pointing to it each time. When you read the poem again, ask children to hold up the numeral card 20 each time you say the word *twenty*. Let children take turns using the numeral frame to isolate each occurrence of the numeral 20 (lines 1 and 5).

3. Ask a volunteer to count out 20 apples and use wall adhesive to affix the apples to the tree. For more practice, place 20 counters on a table near the pocket chart. Have a child count out 20 counters and place them next to a line in the poem that has the numeral 20. Repeat for the other line in the poem with the numeral 20.

4. Write the numeral 20 slowly on chart paper (or a whiteboard) to demonstrate how it is formed. Have children follow your movements by writing the numeral on a partner's back.

5. Give each child a copy of the mini-book and a set of counters. Guide children in completing pages 1–3. (See page 7 for directions.) On page 4 of the mini-book, invite children to draw 20 of something else that grows on a tree (such as pears, oranges, or coconuts). Encourage them to include other sets of 20 in their pictures, such as bees, flowers, and bugs.

6. As an extension, introduce children to the word *twenty*. Write the word on a sentence strip, and trim to size. Add the word card to the pocket chart. Read the word together. Then have children match the word *twenty* to the numeral 20 in the poem and to the corresponding number of counters. Allow time over the next few days for children to revisit the poem and manipulatives.

The Numbers 21–30

You can use the open-ended poem below to teach each of the numbers 21–30.
Complete the poem for the number you are teaching. Modify each step of the lesson accordingly.

Fish, Snails, and Whales

_____ fish swim in the sea.
I can count them easily.
_____ fish all swish their tails,
As they swim past snails and whales.
They swim to the place they like the best.
Then close their eyes and take a rest!

Materials

- pocket chart
- sentence strips
- numeral cards (21–30; pages 158–159)
- picture cards (fish, snail, whale; page 170)
- numeral frame (page 160)
- counters (page 176)
- number practice mini-book (pages 171–172)
- numeral strips (21–30; pages 173, 175)

Getting Ready

1. Copy the title and poem onto sentence strips (one line per sentence strip). Highlight the numeral in lines 1 and 3 (as indicated by the blanks, above). Place the sentence strips in order in the pocket chart.

2. Photocopy a class set plus one extra of the numeral card. Photocopy and cut apart the picture cards (making multiple copies of the fish, snail, and whale to match the number being taught) and counters (varies).

3. Place the picture cards and numeral card (in that order) across the top of the pocket chart. Place the counters to the side.

4. Customize the mini-book for the target numeral (21–30), and make a class set. (See page 7 for directions.)

Teaching With the Pocket Chart Poem

1. Give each child a copy of the numeral card, and then tell children to get ready to listen to a poem about ___ fish. As you read the poem, emphasize the numeral by pointing to it each time (21, 22, and so on). Place the picture cards next to the rhyme accordingly. When you read the poem again, ask children to hold up the numeral card each time you say the number word. Let children take turns using the numeral frame to isolate each occurrence of the numeral (lines 1 and 3).

2. Place ___ counters on a table near the pocket chart. Ask a child to count out ___ counters and place them next to a line in the poem that has the numeral ___. Repeat for the other line in the poem with the numeral ___.

3. Write the lesson's target numeral slowly on chart paper (or a whiteboard) to demonstrate how it is formed. Have children follow your movements by writing the numeral in the air.

4. Give each child a copy of the mini-book and a set of counters. Guide children in completing pages 1–3. (See page 7 for directions.) On page 4 of the mini-book, invite children to draw a picture of the corresponding number of fish. Encourage them to include other sets of objects to represent the same number in their pictures, such as shells, bubbles, and plants.

5. As an extension, introduce children to the number word that goes with the target numeral of the lesson (for example, if you've filled in the rhyme with the numeral 21, teach the number word *twenty-one*). Write the word on a sentence strip, and trim to size. Add the word card to the pocket chart. Read the word together. Then have children match the word to the numeral in the poem and to the corresponding number of counters. Allow time over the next few days for children to revisit the poem and manipulatives.

Activities and Games
for Every Number

Open-Ended Pocket Chart Poem

Write the following poem on sentence strips, writing any numeral in the spaces (use the same number in each of the two spaces):

> It's fun to count our fingers.
> It's fun to count our toes.
> It's fun to count our ears,
> Or even count our nose!
> Today we'll learn the number ___.
> Let's count ___ things right now.
> It will be such fun for me,
> If you would show me how!

After writing a numeral, such as 5, in each blank space, have children use the counters (page 176) to represent that number. Repeat with different numerals.

I Spy

Say to children, "I spy seven crayons," or some other number of objects that can be found in the classroom. Have one child find and count the objects, while another child places the appropriate numeral card and number of counters in the pocket chart. Continue with other objects and numbers. As a variation, let children take turns "spying" numbers of objects for their classmates to find and count.

Guess the Number

Place a group of numeral cards facedown on a table, and have a volunteer select a card. The other children try to guess the number by asking questions such as the following: *Is your numeral greater than 15? Is your numeral less than 20?* After children guess the numeral, another volunteer selects a card and the game continues.

Drum the Number

You will need a toy drum or another musical instrument for this activity. Invite a child to be the drummer and think of a number from 1 to 10. Have the child whisper the number to you and then beat the drum that number of times. Have another child place the appropriate number of counters (and numeral card, if desired) in the pocket chart as the rest of the children write the number at their seats.

Countdown

Have a child place numeral cards 1–10 in the pocket chart in reverse order (from 10 to 1), and count down the numbers aloud, while another child does a second task, such as drawing circles or writing his or her name. How many circles was the second child able to draw during the countdown? Have children switch roles and play again.

Taking Inventory

Choose several classroom items to inventory, such as jars of paint, scissors, and glue sticks. Draw a picture of each item and place the items in a column in the pocket chart. Have partners select an item from the pocket chart, count the items in the classroom, and place the appropriate numeral card next to the picture.

Concentration

Place the numeral cards for 1–10 (or 11–20, or 21–30) facedown in random order in the pocket chart. Make another set of 10 cards that visually represents each number with self-stick stars or circles, and place those cards facedown in random order as well. Have children turn over two cards to see if the numeral matches the number of stars. If the two cards match, the child keeps them. If not, he or she returns them facedown to the same spots. Play continues until all cards have been matched. Children may play independently, with partners, or in small groups.

Blow Your Horn

You will need a horn or something else that creates a sound for this activity. Count aloud slowly. Then stop and replace the next number with the sound of the horn. For example: "*One, two, three, four, five* [blow the horn]." Call on a volunteer to place the numeral card that shows the missing number in the pocket chart as the rest of the children write the numeral. To make the game more challenging, try a sequence in which you continue to count after you blow the horn. For example: "*One, two, three, four, five* [blow the horn], *seven, eight, nine, ten.*"

What's the Number?

Place a series of numeral cards faceup in the pocket chart—for example, 1 through 10. Ask children to close their eyes. Then turn over one of the cards. Ask children to open their eyes and identify the numeral on the card that you turned over. To vary the game, use fewer or more cards, or turn over more than one card.

Point to the Number

Place the numerals 1–30 (or whatever numbers children have learned so far) in a grid in the pocket chart. Place the pocket chart so that it is accessible to children. Invite volunteers to come to the chart, cover their eyes, and put their finger on the chart. When they open their eyes, they tell what number they are pointing to, and then clap and count to that number.

Counting Letters in Names

In the pocket chart, in list form, display the first name of each child. Have each child take a turn at the chart, counting the letters in his or her name, and placing the appropriate numeral card next to the name. Then ask children the following questions: *Which names have the most letters? Which names have the fewest letters? Which names have the same number of letters?* If you wish, you can also use the information from the pocket chart to make a bar graph.

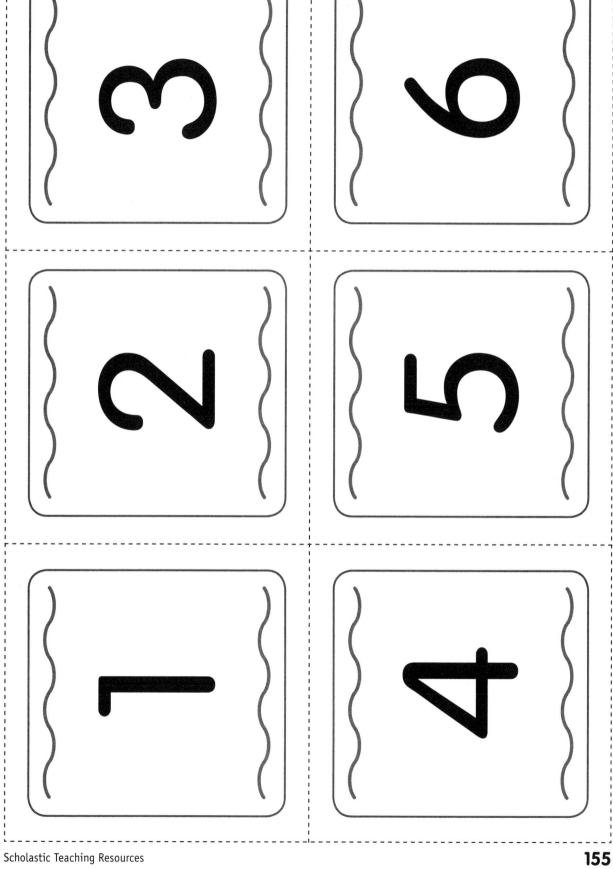

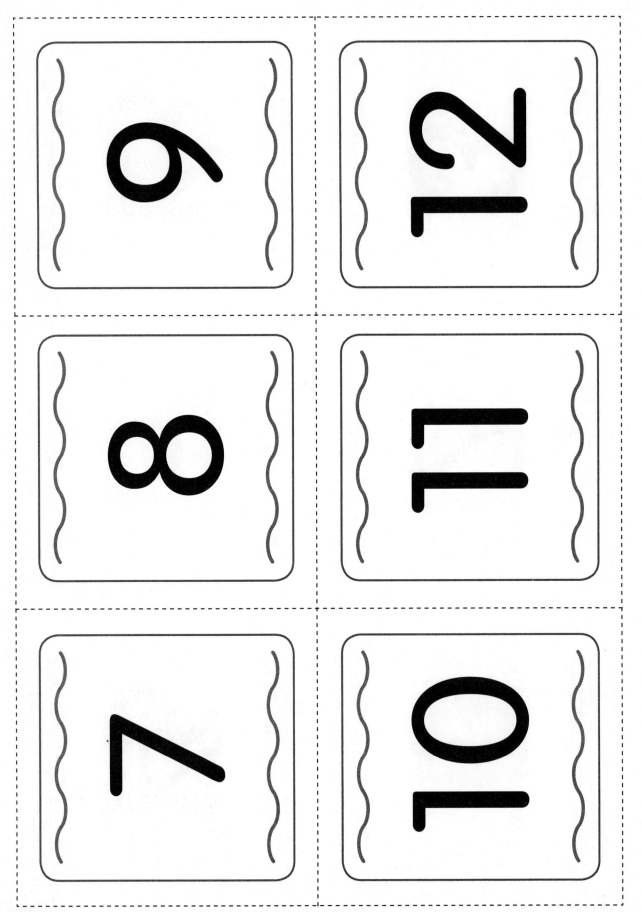

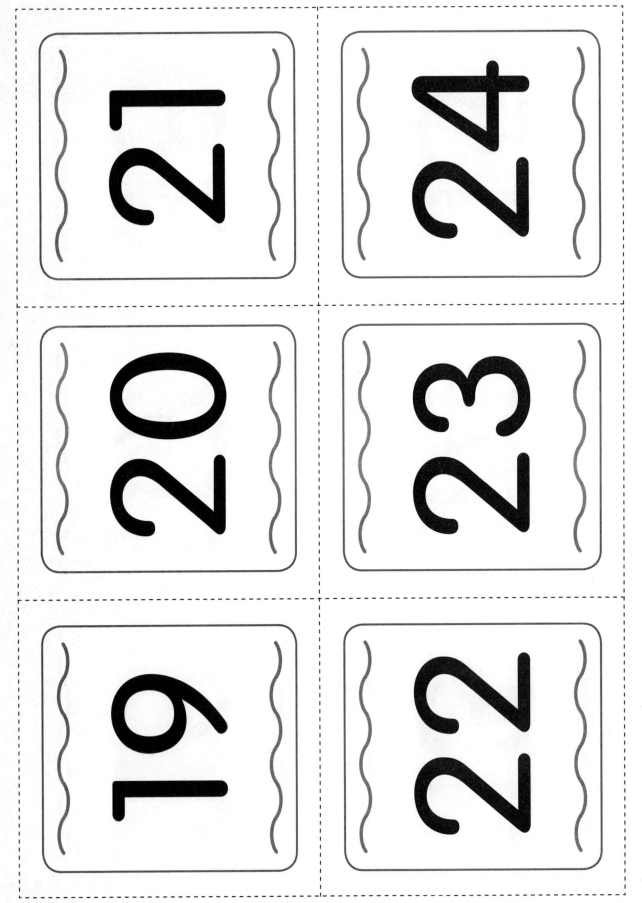

The Big Book of Pocket Chart Poems: ABCs & 123s © 2007 by Linda B. Ross, Scholastic Teaching Resources

Numeral Frame

Cut out.

The Big Book of Pocket Chart Poems: ABCs & 123s © 2007 by Linda B. Ross, Scholastic Teaching Resources

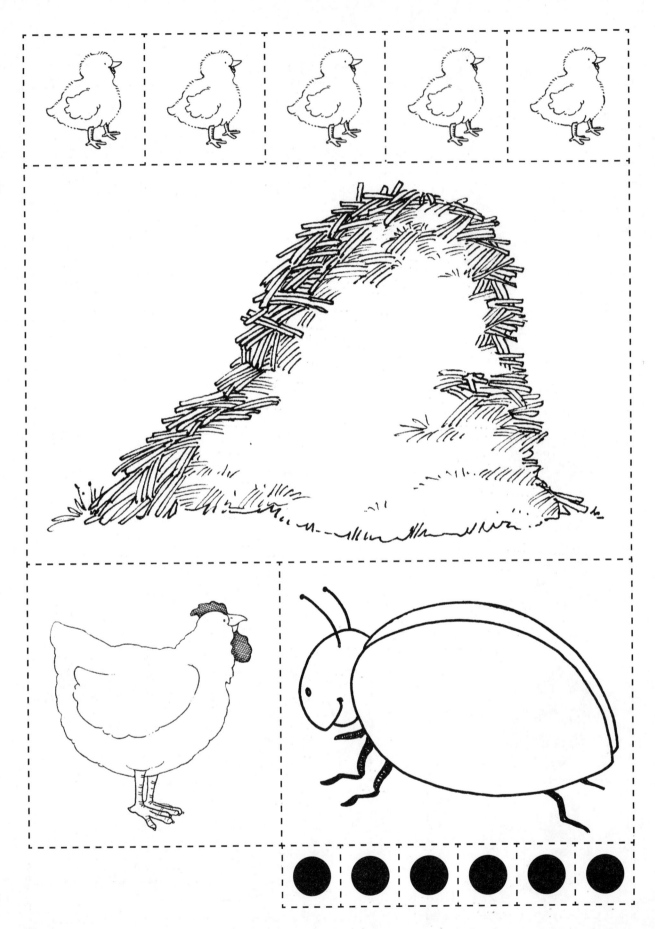

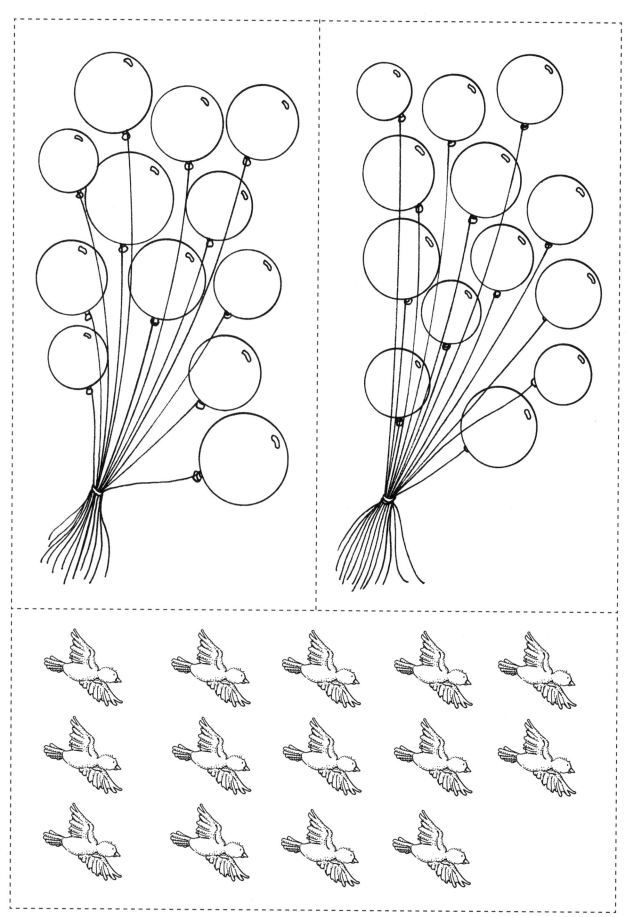

The Big Book of Pocket Chart Poems: ABCs & 123s © 2007 by Linda B. Ross, Scholastic Teaching Resources

123s

My Book About
the Number

Trace the numeral with your finger.

By _____

Date _____

1

123s

Trace the numeral
_____ with a pencil.

Write the numeral _____.

2

123s

I can count to _____.

Use the back of page 2 if you need more room to paste counters.

③

123s

Draw a picture about the number _____.

④

Reproducible Number Strips
Templates for Mini-Book Page 1

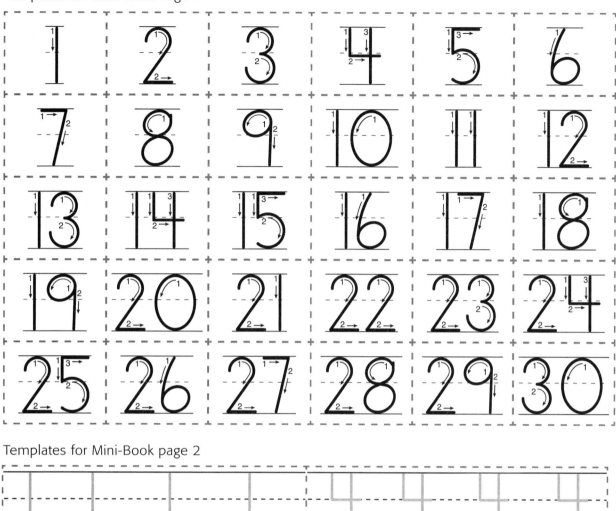

Templates for Mini-Book page 2

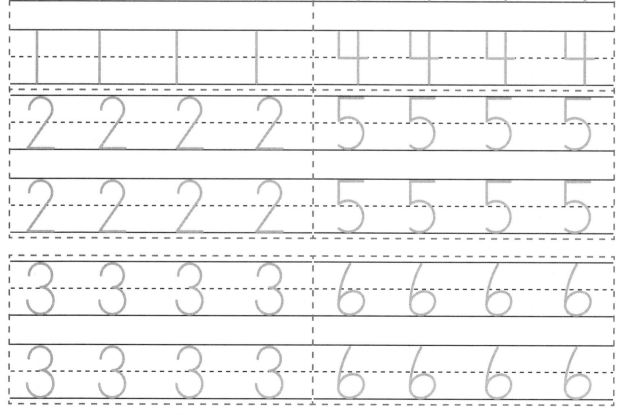

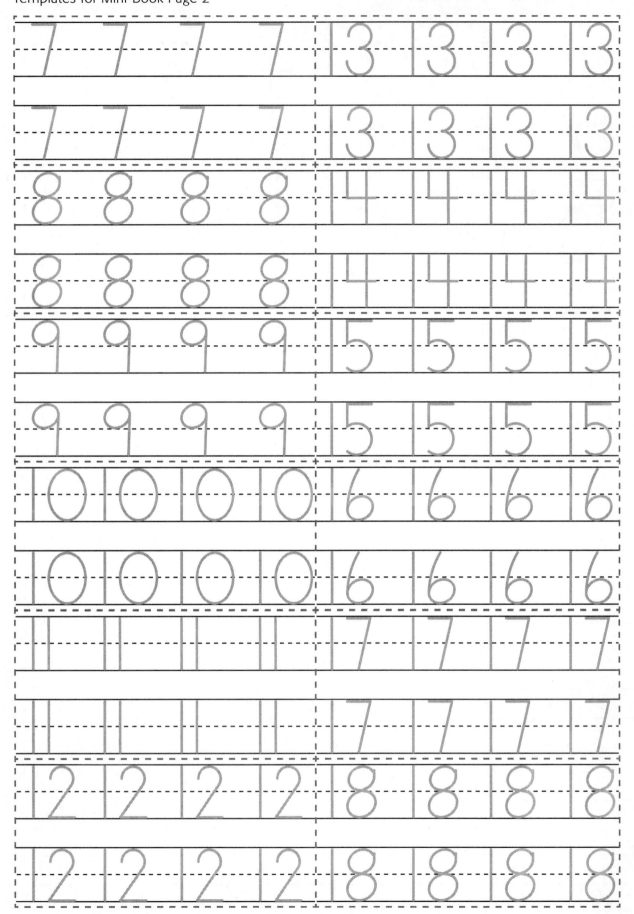

Reproducible Number Strips

Templates for Mini-Book Page 2

19 19 19 19 25 25 25

19 19 19 19 25 25 25

20 20 20 26 26 26

20 20 20 26 26 26

21 21 21 21 27 27 27

21 21 21 21 27 27 27

22 22 22 28 28 28

22 22 22 28 28 28

23 23 23 29 29 29

23 23 23 29 29 29

24 24 24 30 30 30

24 24 24 30 30 30

Reproducible Counters

The Big Book of Pocket Chart Poems: ABCs & 123s © 2007 by Linda B. Ross, Scholastic Teaching Resources